Reading & Vocabulary Development 3

Cause & Effect

Fourth Edition

Patricia Ackert | Linda Lee

NATIONAL GEOGRAPHIC LEARNING | CENGAGE Learning

Australia • Brazil • Japan • Korea • Mexico • Singapore • Spain • United Kingdom • United States

Reading & Vocabulary Development 3:
Cause & Effect, Fourth Edition
Patricia Ackert and Linda Lee

Publisher, Adult and Academic ESL:
  James W. Brown

Senior Acquisitions Editor: Sherrise Roehr

Director of Development: Anita Raducanu

Development Editor: Tom Jefferies

Editorial Assistant: Katherine Reilly

Senior Production Editor: Maryellen E. Killeen

Director of Marketing: Amy Mabley

Marketing Manager: Laura Needham

Senior Print Buyer: Mary Beth Hennebury

Compositor: Pre-Press Company, Inc.

Project Manager: Sally Lifland, Lifland et al.,
  Bookmakers

Photo Researcher: Gail Magin

Illustrator: Barry Burns

Cover Designer: Ha Ngyuen

Text Designer: Quica Ostrander

Library of Congress Control Number 2005921000

ISBN-13: 978-1-4130-0416-8

ISBN: 1-4130-0416-4

ISE ISBN-13: 978-1-4130-0447-2

ISE ISBN: 1-4130-0447-4

National Geographic Learning
20 Channel Center Street
Boston, MA 02210
USA

Cengage Learning is a leading provider of customized learning solutions with office locations around the globe, including Singapore, the United Kingdom, Australia, Mexico, Brazil, and Japan.

Cengage Learning products are represented in Canada by Nelson Education, Ltd.

Visit National Geographic Learning online at **ngl.cengage.com**

Visit our corporate website at **www.cengage.com**

Printed in the United States of America
12 13 14 15 19 18 17 16 15

Contents

To the Instructor   v
Acknowledgments   ix

Unit 1   Explorers   1

Lesson 1   Burke and Wills: Across Australia   2
Lesson 2   Alexandra David-Neel: A French Woman in Tibet   10
Lesson 3   Vitus Bering: Across Siberia to North America   20
Lesson 4   Robert Scott: A Race to the South Pole   29
Lesson 5   Into the Deep: Ocean Exploration   40
Extension Activities
    Video Highlights: CNN Video, *Deep Sea Exploration*   50
    Activity Page: Adventure Trail   52
    Dictionary Page: Understanding Definitions   53

Unit 2   World Issues   55

Lesson 1   World Population Growth   56
Lesson 2   Changes in the Family   68
Lesson 3   Women and Change   78
Lesson 4   Rain Forests   88
Lesson 5   The Garbage Project   98
Extension Activities
    Video Highlights: CNN Video, *Lalita's Story*   107
    Activity Page: Crossword Puzzle   109
    Dictionary Page: Working with Word Forms   110

Unit 3   A Mishmash, or Hodgepodge   111

Lesson 1   Roadrunners   112
Lesson 2   Afraid to Fly   122
Lesson 3   Languages and Language Diversity   132
Lesson 4   Skyscrapers   143
Lesson 5   Left-Handedness   153
Extension Activities
    Video Highlights: CNN Video, *The Green Skyscraper*   163
    Activity Page: Familiar Phrases   165
    Dictionary Page: Understanding Grammar Codes   166

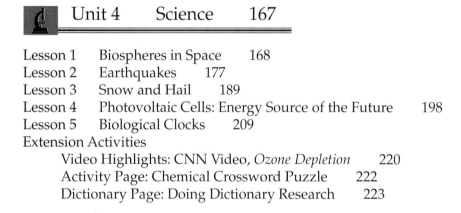

Unit 4   Science   167

Lesson 1   Biospheres in Space   168
Lesson 2   Earthquakes   177
Lesson 3   Snow and Hail   189
Lesson 4   Photovoltaic Cells: Energy Source of the Future   198
Lesson 5   Biological Clocks   209
Extension Activities
    Video Highlights: CNN Video, *Ozone Depletion*   220
    Activity Page: Chemical Crossword Puzzle   222
    Dictionary Page: Doing Dictionary Research   223

Unit 5   Medicine and Health   225

Lesson 1   Headaches   226
Lesson 2   Sleep and Dreams   236
Lesson 3   Health Care and Epidemics   246
Lesson 4   Medicine: From Leeches to Lasers   258
Lesson 5   Cholesterol and Heart Disease   268
Extension Activities
    Video Highlights: CNN Video, *The Singing Doctor*   281
    Activity Page: Who Said What?   283
    Dictionary Page: Learning About Word Stress   285

Vocabulary   287
Skills Index   291

Reading & Vocabulary Development 3: Cause & Effect is a best-selling beginning reading skills text designed for students of English as a second or foreign language who have a basic vocabulary in English of about 1,300 words. This text teaches about 700 more words.

Cause & Effect is one in a series of reading skills texts. The complete series has been designed to meet the needs of students from the beginning to the high intermediate levels and includes the following:

Reading & Vocabulary Development 1: Facts & Figures
Reading & Vocabulary Development 2: Thoughts & Notions
Reading & Vocabulary Development 3: Cause & Effect
Reading & Vocabulary Development 4: Concepts & Comments

In addition to the student text, an answer key, VHS, DVD, audio cassette, and audio CD are also available. *Cause & Effect* uses the following methodology:

- **Theme-based approach to reading.** Each of the five units has a theme such as world issues, science, or health.

- **Systematic presentation and recycling of vocabulary.** One of the primary tasks of students is developing a useful and personally relevant vocabulary base. In *Cause & Effect,* up to 24 words are introduced in each lesson. These words appear in boldface type. Those underlined are illustrated or glossed in the margin. All of the new vocabulary items are used several times in the lesson, and then are systematically recycled throughout the text.

- **Pedagogical design.** The central goal of *Cause & Effect* is to help students develop the critical reading skills they will need for academic, personal, and/or career purposes. By any standard, the range of exercise types in *Cause & Effect* is rich and varied. This text provides students with practice in comprehension, building vocabulary, making inferences, finding the main idea, determining cause and effect, scanning, summarizing, paraphrasing, understanding the sequence of events, and learning to work more effectively with two-word verbs, compound words, connecting words, and noun substitutes.

 ## Organization of *Cause & Effect*

Cause & Effect is organized into five units. Each unit contains five lessons packed with exercises and activities.

• **"Before You Read" Questions.** These pre-reading questions provide a motivation for reading the text.

• **Context Clues.** A context clue exercise at the beginning of each lesson introduces some of the vocabulary for the following lesson. This section is designed to pre-teach particularly important vocabulary items.

• **Vocabulary.** The first two exercises give practice with new words in a different context but with the same meaning.

• **Vocabulary Review.** Vocabulary items are used in subsequent texts and exercises to give additional review. They are fill-ins or matching synonyms and antonyms.

• **Comprehension.** First is a set of true/false, true/false/not enough information, or multiple choice questions. Then come comprehension questions, which include inference and discussion questions. The comprehension questions may also be given as written assignments.

• **Main Idea.** Students must choose the main idea of a paragraph from three possibilities.

• **Word Study.** A selection of word study exercises is provided at the end of each lesson. It reinforces structural points, such as verb forms, two-word verbs, and articles, that the students are learning in other classes. It also gives spelling rules for noun plurals and verb endings. Later units have charts of word forms. The exercises are not intended to be complete explanations and practice of the grammar points.

• **Writing.** Each lesson closes with a writing exercise.

- **Extension Activities.** Each unit ends with a set of high-interest, interactive tasks to help students practice the new vocabulary and the skills they have learned in more open-ended contexts.

CNN Video Highlights—The highlight of each set of extension activities is a short video-based lesson centered on a stimulating, authentic clip from the CNN video archives. Each video lesson follows the same sequence of activities:

Before You Watch encourages students to recall background knowledge based on their own experiences or from information presented in the readings.

As You Watch asks students to watch for general information such as the topic of the clip.

After You Watch gets the students to expand on the main points of the video by establishing further connections to the reading passages, their own experiences, and their ideas and opinions.

Activity Page—Games found on this page encourage students to practice the vocabulary and structures found in that unit's lessons in a relaxed, open-ended way.

Dictionary Page—Exercises on this page offer students practice with dictionary skills based on entries from *The Newbury House Dictionary of American English.*

- **Skills Index.** This index provides teachers and students with a handy reference for all of the reading and writing skills introduced in *Cause & Effect,* as well as all of the grammatical structures found in the text.

 New to This Edition

The best-selling reading series just got better! The fourth edition of *Cause & Effect* contains new readings, new pedagogy, and new ancillaries.

- Four fresh new readings engage students in fascinating new topics. The new readings for this edition are as follows:

  Unit 1, Lesson 5: Into the Deep: Ocean Exploration
  Unit 2, Lesson 5: The Garbage Project
  Unit 3, Lesson 3: Languages and Language Diversity
  Unit 5, Lesson 4: Medicine: From Leeches to Lasers

- Thoroughly updated and checked for factual accuracy, each reading has been revised to include level-appropriate structures and vocabulary.

- New pedagogical design, photos, and illustrations aid student comprehension and ease navigation through the text.

- *ExamView® Pro* test-generating software allows instructors to create custom tests and quizzes.

- A new website (found at elt.heinle.com/readingandvocabulary) features vocabulary flashcards, cross-word puzzles, quizzes, and more to help students review for tests.

Acknowledgments

The authors and publisher would like to thank the following individuals who offered helpful feedback and suggestions for the revision of the *Reading & Vocabulary Development* series:

Brian Altano—Bergen Community College, Paramus, NJ

Benjamin Deleon—Delano High School, Delano, CA

Elaine Dow—Quinsigamond Community College, Worcester, MA

Julia Karet—Chaffey College, Rancho Cucamonga, CA

Jane Sitko—Edmonds Community College, Lynnwood, WA

Explorers

*One doesn't discover new lands without consenting
to lose sight of the shore for a very long time.*
—André Gide

© Lightscapes Photography, Inc./CORBIS

lesson
1

Burke and Wills: Across Australia

© Howard Davies./CORBIS

Before You Read

1. What information about Australia do the map and the photograph give you?

2. Is Australia larger or smaller than your country?

3. What else do you know about Australia?

1 Burke and Wills: Across Australia

Australia is a huge country, and the outback (the Australian word for the **interior** of the country) is desert. In some years, it rains only eight centimeters in the outback, but in other years, rainstorms **turn** the
5 desert **into** sandy swamps.

    Until the eighteenth century, only **aborigines** lived in Australia. These are the first people who lived in Australia. When Europeans went there to live, they **built** towns on the coast. However, in the 1850s, people
10 began thinking more about the interior.

    In 1860, Robert O'Hara Burke, a police officer from Ireland, was **chosen** to lead an **expedition** across the continent from south to north. He took with him William John Wills and eleven other men, camels,
15 horses, and enough **supplies** for a year and a half. They left Melbourne for the Gulf of Carpentaria on August 20, winter in the southern **hemisphere**.

    The expedition had problems from the beginning. Burke had no experience in the outback. The men fought
20 and would not follow **orders**. Twice they left some of their supplies so that they could move faster and later sent one of the men, William Wright, back for them.

    Finally, a small group led by Burke moved on ahead of the others to a river named Cooper's Creek and set up
25 their **base** camp. They were **halfway** across the continent, but it was summer now, with very hot weather and sandstorms.

    They waited a month for Wright, and then Burke decided that four from his small group, with three
30 months' supplies, should travel the 1,250 kilometers to the north coast as quickly as possible. They told the others to wait for them at Cooper's Creek.

    The journey across the desert was very difficult, but at the end of January, they reached the Flinders River

inside; away from the coast

turn into = change (something); become

past participle of *choose*

food and other necessary things

half of the Earth or any other sphere

commands; directions

at last

35 near the Gulf of Carpentaria. They started their return
   journey, but now it was the rainy season and traveling
   was slow and even more difficult than on their trip
   north. They did not have enough food, and the men
   became hungry and sick. Then one of them died. Some
40 of the camels died or were killed for food.

   Finally, on April 21, they arrived back at Cooper's
   Creek, only to find that no one was there. The rest of the
   expedition had left the day before because they thought
   Burke must be dead.

45 The men continued south, but without enough food,
   both Burke and Wills died. Aborigines helped the last
   man who was still alive, and a **search party** found him   a group of people
   in September 1861. He was half crazy from hunger and   who look for
   loneliness.   someone who is lost

50 There were many reasons that the expedition did not
   go as planned. It had an inexperienced leader, the men
   made bad decisions, some did not follow orders, and
   they did not **get along.** But it was the first expedition to   be friendly;
   cross Australia, and Burke and Wills are still known as   not fight
55 **heroes** of **exploration.**

a Vocabulary

In this book, difficult words are repeated several times in the exercises. These words are also repeated and reviewed in other lessons. It is not necessary to list new English words with their meanings in your own language. You will learn them just by practicing. In each lesson, when you read the text the first time, underline the words you don't know. Then you can give yourself a test when you finish the lesson. Look at the words you underlined and see if you understand them. If you don't know them yet, this is the time to memorize them.

In the Vocabulary exercises in this book, write the correct word in each blank. Use a word only once. Use capital letters where they are necessary.

exploration	built	hemisphere	halfway
finally	orders	expedition	loneliness
aborigines	gets along	base	heroes

1. The captain of a ship gives _____orders_____, and the sailors must follow them.

2. In baseball, a player hits the ball and runs to first _____base__ey____.

3. The first Australians are called _____aborigines_____.

4. Most of the Earth has been explored. Now we are in the age of space _____exploration_____, searching for more information about the stars, the moon, and other planets besides Earth.

5. Kumiko _____gets along_____ well with everyone. She is always nice and never fights with people.

6. We _____built_____ our new home from the wood and stone on our land.

7. _____Loneliness_____ is a common feeling when you are far from your friends and family.

8. Asia is in the northern _____hemisphere_____.

9. The writer Jane Austen said, "_____Halfway_____ doings never prosper." I think she meant that it's important to complete things.

10. People who win in the Olympic Games are _____heroes_____ in their countries.

b Vocabulary

Do this exercise the same way you did Exercise a.

- ✓ chosen
- build
- ✓ searching
- ✓ expedition
- ✓ interior
- ✓ supplies
- ✓ party
- got along
- swamps
- ✓ explored
- ✓ finally
- ✓ turned into

1. Burke and Wills led an __expedition__ into the interior of Australia.
2. The explorer Christopher Columbus was __searching__ for a new way to go to India.
3. Burke and Wills __explored__ the interior of Australia.
4. Birds like to live in __swamps__ because there is a lot of water and food.
5. We use one kind of paint for the __interior__ of a house and another kind for the exterior.
6. After three days of driving, I __finally__ arrived at the coast.
7. A search __party__ was sent to find the Burke and Wills expedition.
8. The president of the United States is __chosen__ by the people who vote:
9. The secretary ordered paper, pens, and other __supplies__ for the office.
10. Carlos started to study hard, and he eventually __turned into__ a good student.

c   True/False

*Write **T** if the sentence is true. Write **F** if it is false. If a sentence is false, change it to make it true or explain why it is false. An asterisk (*) before an item means that the answer is either an **inference** or an **opinion**. You cannot find the answer in a sentence in the text. You have to think about the information in the text and things you already know and then decide on the answer.*

_F_ 1. The first Europeans in Australia built villages in the outback *towns on the coast* *lines 8-10* because there were too many aborigines on the coast.

_T_ 2. The Burke and Wills expedition crossed Australia from south to north.

_T_ *3. December is a summer month in Australia.

_F_ 4. Much of the interior of Australia is swampy all year long. *line 4-5*

_T_ 5. Eleven men crossed Australia with Burke and Wills.

_T_ *6. Burke and Wills did not have enough food for their journey back to Cooper's Creek because the rain slowed them down.

_T_ *7. The aborigines could help the last man still alive because they understood how to live in the desert.

_F_ 8. Burke was a good leader for this expedition. *line 51-52, 19*

d   Comprehension Questions

*Answer these questions in complete sentences. An asterisk (*) means that the answer is either an **inference** or an **opinion**. You cannot find the exact answer in the text.*

1. Where did the first Europeans live when they went to Australia?
*2. Why were camels good animals for this expedition?
3. Why did the men leave some of their supplies behind?
4. Why was it difficult to travel in the interior of Australia?
5. What happened to some of the camels?
6. Give two reasons why this expedition had so many problems.
*7. Do you think Burke and Wills should be called heroes of exploration? Why?

Lesson 1: Burke and Wills: Across Australia

e   Main Idea

What is the main idea of paragraph 4 (lines 18–22)?

a. Robert Burke led this expedition.
b. The expedition had many problems.
c. Burke had no experience in the outback.

f   Two-Word Verbs

English has many two-word verbs. Each of the two words is easy, but when they are put together, they mean something different. There is often no way to guess what they mean. You have to learn each one.

Learn these two-word verbs and then fill in the blanks with the right words. Use the correct verb form.

turn into	=	change (something) into; become
get along (with)	=	not fight; be friendly
break down	=	stop going or working (often said about a car)
call on	=	ask (someone) to speak (as when a teacher asks a student to speak)
put away	=	put (something) in the place where it belongs

1. Our washing machine _broke down_ yesterday, and I couldn't finish washing my clothes.
2. Tommy and his little brother don't _get along_ very well. They fight about something almost every day.
3. Ali knew the answer when the teacher _called on_ him.
4. It was rainy this morning, but now it has _turned into_ a beautiful day.
5. Mary doesn't usually _put away_ her clothes. She just leaves them on a chair or the bed.

g Articles: A, An, The

There are so many rules about articles that it is easier just to get used to them by practicing than to learn all the rules. However, you will learn a few of the rules later in this book.

Here are some sentences or parts of sentences from the text. Put an article in the blank if it is necessary.

1. In other years, rainstorms turn _the_ desert into sandy swamps.
2. Until _the_ eighteenth century, only aborigines lived in Australia.
3. In 1860, _____ Robert O'Hara Burke, _a_ police officer from Ireland, was chosen to lead _an_ expedition across _the_ continent from south to north.
4. He took with him William John Wills and eleven other men, _____ camels, _____ horses, and enough supplies for _a_ year and _a_ half.
5. _The_ expedition had problems from _the_ beginning.
6. _The_ men fought and would not follow _____ orders.

h Guided Writing

Write one of these two short compositions.

1. You are the last person still alive from the Burke and Wills expedition. It is September 1861, and the search party has just found you. Tell them what happened to you.
2. You are the leader of another expedition across Australia. Explain what you will do differently.

Alexandra David-Neel: A French Woman in Tibet

← stick
staff — konae

© Wason Collection on East Asia, Cornell University Library

Before You Read

1. What do you know about the history and geography of Tibet?

2. What information does the photograph give you about Alexandra David-Neel?

3. Alexandra David-Neel traveled alone to Tibet in the early twentieth century. What do you think her goal was?

Context Clues

It is not necessary to look up every new word in the dictionary. You can often tell what a word means from the sentence it is in or from the sentences after it. For example, the word **aborigines** in line 6 on page 3 is explained in the next sentence. Take a look. What are aborigines? Always look for context clues when you are reading. Try not to look up every new word in your dictionary.

*The words in **bold** print below are from this lesson. Use context clues to guess what each word means. Do all of the Context Clues exercises in the book this way.*

1. David-Neel was very unhappy when she was a child. She **escaped** her unhappiness by reading books on adventure and travel.

2. Later, she studied the Buddhist religion and wrote **articles** and books about it.

3. In 1903, she started working as a **journalist,** writing articles about Asia and Buddhism for English and French magazines and newspapers.

4. She wrote her husband long letters full of **details** about her travels.

5. For centuries, Tibet was a **secret** and mysterious place to the rest of the world. Only a few foreigners were able to visit the area.

2 Alexandra David-Neel: A French Woman in Tibet

Tibet has been a **secret** and mysterious place to the rest of the world for several centuries. It is on a high plateau in Asia, **surrounded** by even higher mountains, and only a few foreigners were able to cross its **borders** until recently.

legal lines between countries

5 One of these foreigners was a French woman named Alexandra David-Neel (1868–1969). She traveled by herself in India, China, and Tibet. She studied the Buddhist religion, wrote **articles** and books about it, and collected ancient Buddhist books. She also became
10 a Buddhist herself.

David-Neel always said she had an unhappy **childhood**. She **escaped** her unhappiness by reading books on adventure and travel. She **ran away** from school several times and even ran away to England
15 when she was only 16.

left without telling anyone

She was a singer for several years, but in 1903 she started working as a **journalist,** writing articles about Asia and Buddhism for English and French magazines and newspapers. The next year, when she was 37, she married
20 Philippe-François Neel. It was an unusual marriage. After five days together, they moved to different cities and never lived together again. Yet he **supported** her all his life, and she wrote him hundreds of long letters full of **details** about her travels.

gave (her) money to live on

25 She traveled all over Europe and North Africa, but she went to India in 1911 to study Buddhism, and then her **real** travels began. She traveled in India and also in Nepal and Sikkim, the small countries north of India in the Himalaya Mountains, but her goal was Tibet. She
30 continued to study Buddhism and learned to speak Tibetan. She traveled to villages and religious centers, with only an interpreter and a few men to carry her camping equipment. For several months, she lived in a **cave** in Sikkim and studied Buddhism and the Tibetan

cave

35   language. Then she **adopted** a 15-year-old Sikkimese
boy to travel with her. He **remained** with her until   **stayed**
his death at the age of 55.

     For the next seven years, she traveled in **remote**   **far from towns**
areas of China. These were years of **civil war** in China,   **war between people**
40 and she was often in danger. She traveled for   **in the same country**
thousands of kilometers on horseback with only a few
men to help her—through desert heat and sandstorms
and the rain, snow, and freezing **temperatures** of the
colder areas.

        beggar

45   In 1924, David-Neel was 56 years old. She darkened
her skin and dressed as an old **beggar**. She carried only
a beggar's bowl and a backpack and traveled through
hot lowlands and snowy mountain passes until she
reached the border of Tibet. Because she spoke Tibetan
50 so well, she was able to cross the border and reach the
famous city of Lhasa without anyone knowing that she
was European and forbidden to be there. It was often
freezing cold, and sometimes there wasn't enough food.
Sometimes she was sick, and once she nearly died. This
55 was the most dangerous of all her journeys, but she
reached her goal and collected more information about
Tibetan Buddhism.

     She returned to France in 1925. She spent several
years writing about her **research** and adventures and   **search for new**
60 translating ancient Tibetan religious books. When she   **information**
was 66, she returned to China and the Tibetan border
area for ten years. In 1944, the Second World War
reached even that remote area, and at the age of 76, she
walked for days, sometimes without food, until she was
65 able to reach a place from which she could fly to India
and then home to France. She continued writing and
translating until she died, just seven weeks before her
101st birthday.

     Most explorers traveled to discover and map new
70 places. David-Neel went to do research on Buddhism.
She said that freedom was the most important thing in
life for her, and, **like** many other explorers, she lived a   **similar to**
dangerous, exciting, free life.

a   Vocabulary

Write the correct word in each blank. Use a word only once, and use capital letters if they are necessary.

civil war	temperature	like	border
childhood	article	secret	beggars
caves	journalist	remote	remained

1. We didn't tell him about his birthday party. We wanted it to be
   a ___secret___.
2. There is an interesting ___article___ in the newspaper today
   about Tibet.
3. You can find ___beggars___ asking for money in most countries.
4. She lived in Asia when she was an adult, but she spent her
   ___childhood___ in England.
5. Some ancient North Americans lived in ___caves___. Others
   built houses.
6. Normal body ___temperature___ is 98.6 degrees Fahrenheit.
7. She went to India in 1911 and ___remained___ there for several years.
8. In the United States, the northern states and the southern states fought a
   ___civil war___ that lasted from 1861 to 1865.
9. The Himalayas are on the ___border___ between China and India.
10. A ___journalist___ collects information and then writes articles about
    it for magazines and newspapers.

b   Vocabulary

Remember to underline the words you don't know as you read the text, and then test yourself when you finish the lesson.

remote	escaped	like	real
details	surrounded	support	journalist
adopted	research	borders	ran away from

1. Everyone calls her Ellie, but her ___real___ name is Elizabeth.
2. Our house is cool in hot weather because it is ___surrounded___ by
   big trees.

3. Nepal, _like_ Tibet, is in the Himalaya Mountains.
4. Mr. and Mrs. Thompson _adopted_ a baby because they couldn't have children of their own.
5. He _ran away from_ school when he was 15 years old and joined the navy. _qaros_
6. Most English paragraphs have a main idea and supporting _details_.
7. Parents usually _support_ their children until the children finish school. The parents pay for everything the children need.
8. Dr. Garcia is doing _research_ for space exploration. _adventures_
9. Her friends live in a _borders_ part of Alaska. The only way to get there is
   by plane.
10. A snake _escaped_ from the zoo last night. If you see it, call the police immediately.

C   Multiple Choice

Circle the letter of the best answer. An asterisk (*) means that the answer is an inference or opinion. You cannot find the answer in a sentence in the text.

1. Alexandra David-Neel went to Asia to __A__.
   a. study Buddhism   _line 26_
   b. lead an expedition
   c. adopt a son

2. When she was a child, she read to __B__.
   a. become a Buddhist
   b. escape her unhappiness   _line 12-13_
   c. learn about Europe

3. After she got married, __B__.
   a. she lived in Europe with her husband for several years
   b. her husband supported her
   c. her husband traveled in Europe with her   _line 22-23_

*4. It is possible that she __A, C__.
   a. took photographs during her travels
   b. had a car when she lived in a cave
   c. spoke Tibetan to her Indian friends

5. The place she wanted most to visit was __C__.
   a. India
   b. China
   c. Tibet

   line 29

6. Her travels in China were dangerous because __A__.
   a. there was a civil war
   b. she was traveling on horseback
   c. she was a beggar

   line 39

7. David-Neel said that __B__.
   a. she wasn't afraid of danger
   b. freedom was very important to her
   c. she wanted her husband to travel with her

   line 71

d Comprehension Questions

Always answer the comprehension questions with complete sentences.

1. Why is Tibet a mysterious place? Because Tibet surrounded by even higher mountans.
*2. Why did David-Neel run away from school?
3. What is a journalist? Who writes artickles in newspapers and magazines
4. What was unusual about her marriage? She lived indepence from her husband
5. What did she do when she was living in a cave? Studied Buddhism, and langvage Tibetan.
6. What does *remote areas* mean? far away from towns
7. Why didn't the Tibetans know she was a foreigner? Because she looked like Tibetan woman
8. What kind of work did she do after her last trip? Continued writing and transtating.
*9. Do you think she lived a free life? Why? Yes, because she found what she escaped

e Main Idea

What is the main idea of paragraph 3 (lines 11–15)?

a. David-Neel read books on travel and adventure.
b. David-Neel ran away from school several times.
c. David-Neel had an unhappy childhood.

Word Forms

Choose a word form from line 1 of the chart to use in sentence 1, and so on. Use the right verb forms and singular or plural nouns. There are empty spaces on the chart because there are not four forms for every word.

	Verb	Noun	Adjective	Adverb
1.	adopt	adoption	adopted	
2.	surround	surroundings	surrounding	
3.	beg	beggar		
4.		hero	heroic	heroically
5.	remain *осабаное* *stay*	remainder *left over* *остаюге (chicken parts)* remains *(dead body)*	remaining	
6.	supply *носсалоеѕ*	supply *носсабаеа*	supplied *носоуоущееі*	
7.	explore	exploration		
8.	secrete	secret	secretive	secretly
9.		reality	real	really
10.	choose	choice	choice	

1. Many ___adopted (adj)___ children want to meet their birth parents.

2. Dan drove so fast on his vacation trip that he hardly saw his ___surroundings (n)___.

3. Small children often ___beg (v)___ to go with their parents when the parents go out at night.

4. Jumping into the freezing water to save the child was a ___heroic (adj)___ action.

5. They ate half the chicken and put the ___remainder (n)___ in the refrigerator for the next day.

6. The company was unable to ___supply (v)___ most of the things we ordered.

7. Are you more interested in the ___exploration (n)___ of outer space or the Earth's oceans?

The police found the remains on the river.

Lesson 2: Alexandra David-Neel

8. I don't know why my children are being so _secretive (adj)_ today. Usually they like to tell me where they are going.
9. Can you help me? I'm _really (adv)_ having trouble with this computer.
10. I can't decide which movie to see. You make the _choice (n)_ .

g Articles

A and **an** are used to show that the noun after it is one of a group.

John Burke was **an** explorer. (He was one of many explorers throughout history.)

Maria is **a** student. (She is one of many students in the world.)

I took **an** apple out of the refrigerator. (It is one of many apples in the world.)

The is used to show that the noun is one special, particular, specific case of the noun or nouns.

John Burke and William John Wills were **the** first explorers to cross Australia.

Maria is **the** best student in the class.

I took **the** apple out of the refrigerator. (There was only one apple in the refrigerator.)

Put the right article in the blanks.

1. Australia is _a_ huge country.
2. _The_ journalist who wrote this article is a friend of mine.
3. David-Neel was _a_ journalist.
4. Please close _the_ door.
5. Her office is _the_ first one on the left.
6. _A_ professor called you today, but I don't know who it was.
7. Who was _the_ worst teacher you ever had?

h Compound Words

Compound words are common in English. They are two words put together, and the meaning of the compound word is related to the meanings of the two words. They are not like two-word verbs, whose meaning is different from the meaning of each word by itself.

Put these compound words in the right blanks in the sentences below.

horseback	sandstorm	snowstorm	keyhole
mailbox	sidewalk	doorbell	weekend

1. Barbara couldn't drive to her parents' house last week because there was a bad _snowstorm_ , and it was very cold.
2. Abdullah looks in his _mailbox_ every day, and he usually finds a letter.
3. A _sidewalk_ is a place for people to walk at the side of the street.
4. When you unlock a door, you put your key in the _keyhole_ .
5. The _doorbell_ rang, and Susan went to open the door.
6. Did you ever go _weekend_ riding?

i Guided Writing

Write one of these two short compositions.

1. You are Alexandra David-Neel. Write a letter to your husband. Describe one or two of your adventures in some detail. Add your own ideas about what you saw, heard, tasted, touched, or smelled.
2. Describe an adventure you had or an unusual trip you took. Use details about what you saw, heard, tasted, touched, or smelled.

Lesson 2: Alexandra David-Neel

lesson 3

Vitus Bering: Across Siberia to North America

© Jacques Langevin/CORBIS SYGMA

Before You Read

1. How can you get from Siberia to Alaska? *on Airplane or on a boat*

2. What is the name of the body of water between Siberia and Alaska? *Bering Sea*

3. Which are longer in Siberia and Alaska, winters or summers?
   winters

Context Clues

You can often guess the meaning of a word from the sentence, even if the sentence doesn't explain the word exactly. For example, in this lesson, one sentence says, "They lost a lot of food when one of the ships **sank** in a storm." What could a storm do to a ship so that the food was lost? The ship probably went down into the water to the bottom of the ocean. When you can guess easily what a word means from the sentence, don't look up the word in your dictionary.

*Now practice with these new words from this lesson. Use context clues to guess what each **bold** word means.*

1. Vitus Bering wanted to explore the east coast of Siberia and to find out if Asia and North America were **joined.**

2. Bering made careful plans for his trip, but there were many **delays.** Because of this, he had only one summer to explore the area instead of two years.

3. Bering's expedition **gathered** important scientific information about the interior of Siberia.

4. When scientists read Bering's reports, they **realized** that he was a great explorer.

5. The water between Siberia and Alaska is now called the Bering Sea to **remind** us of this great explorer.

3   Vitus Bering: Across Siberia to North America

In 1733, the most complete scientific expedition in history up to that time left St. Petersburg, Russia. The goal of the expedition was to explore the east coast of Siberia and to find out if Asia and North America were
5 **joined.** The scientists planned to report on everything: the **geography**, climate, plants, animals, and customs and languages of the Siberian people.

    The expedition had to cross Siberia **in order to** reach the Pacific Ocean. Vitus Bering, the leader of the whole
10 expedition, left St. Petersburg with almost 600 people. The group **included** a few scientists, **skilled** workers of all kinds, **soldiers**, and sailors. Alexei Chirikov left later, with most of the scientists and **tons** of supplies.

    It took seven years for Bering's and Chirikov's groups
15 to cross Siberia. They traveled mostly in flat-bottomed boats on the rivers. Bering's group spent a year in Tobolsk, where they built a ship and explored the Ob River. They continued to Yakutsk, where they spent four years. Yakutsk was only a small village and there were
20 many people in the expedition, so they had to build their own buildings. They also built boats and explored the Lena River. Then they moved on to Okhotsk on the eastern coast. It took two more years to build ships so that they could explore and map the east coast.

25   Bering made careful plans, but there were always problems. For example, they lost a lot of their food when one of the ships sank in a storm. But finally, their two ships started for North America. They had only one summer instead of two years for their explorations
30 because of the many problems and **delays.** And summers are short in the north.

    There was more bad luck. There were storms, and the two ships lost contact, but at last the sailors on

connected

the way parts of a place are positioned within it

to

had in it

people in the military

unit of measure-ment; in the U.S., 2,000 pounds = 1 ton

22

Bering's ship saw mountains a short distance across the
35 sea. This **proved** that North America and Asia were two
separate continents.   different

   Their problems continued. Their water supply was
low, but when the men went **ashore** in Alaska, they got
water that was a little salty. Many of the men were sick
40 from scurvy, a disease caused by the **lack** of **vitamin** C.   not having enough
When they drank the salty water, they became even
sicker. Then they started dying, one after another.

   As the ship sailed south, back toward Okhotsk, it
became lost in storms. Finally, a storm drove it onto a
45 small island, and the men knew their ship could not sail
again. They were in a place with no trees, but there were
birds and animals for food, and **fresh** water to drink.
However, it was too late for many of them. Men
continued to die from scurvy, and on December 8, 1741,
50 Bering died and was buried on the island that is now
named for him. When spring came, the few remaining
men were able to build a small ship from the wood in
the old one and leave the island.

   By this time, the Russian government had lost interest
55 in the North Pacific. Bering's reports were sent back to St.
Petersburg and forgotten. **Decades** later, people **realized**   periods of ten years
that Bering was a great explorer. His expedition **gathered** — meet, get together
important scientific information about the interior of
Siberia, made maps of the eastern coast, and discovered a
60 new part of North America. Today, we have the Bering
Sea between Siberia and Alaska to **remind** us of the   make (us)
leader of this great scientific expedition.   remember

Lesson 3: Vitus Bering: Across Siberia to North America

a Vocabulary

~joined   realize   ~included   ~separate   gather   ~delay
- prove   ~geography   ~remind   ~soldiers   ~lack   ~tons

1. The dancers got in a circle and ___joined___ hands.
2. Did you study the ___geography___ of your country in school?
3. Mr. and Mrs. Baker drive to work in ___separate___ cars because they work in different places.
4. Please ___remind___ me to buy some bread, or I might forget.
5. In some restaurants, the waiter's or waitress's tip is ___included___ in the bill. In others, you leave it separately.
6. Two ___tons___ equals 4,000 U.S. pounds.
7. There will be a short ___delay___ because the chemistry professor needs to get the equipment ready.
8. He didn't ___realize___ what time it was, and he got to class late.
9. ___Soldiers___ have to wear uniforms and follow orders.
10. Burke's expedition failed partly because of his ___lack___ of experience in the Australian outback.

b Vocabulary

~proved   delay   ~decade   ~in order to   ~includes   ~gathered
~ashore   ~fresh   ~skilled   ~separate   ~vitamin   reminder

1. Ali is studying English ___in order to___ go to an American university.
2. Early explorers ___proved___ that the Earth was round and not flat.
3. Ann ___gathered___ up her books and papers and left the library.
4. Scurvy is caused by a lack of ___Vitamin___ C. It was a problem on long ocean trips because sailors didn't have fruit and vegetables to eat.
5. Haiti and the Dominican Republic are parts of the same island, but they are ___separate___ countries.
6. A century is 100 years. A ___decade___ is 10 years.
7. Electricians and mechanics are ___skilled___ workers.
8. After a half hour in the water, the children walked ___ashore___ and dried off.

24

9. People cannot drink sea water. They need ___fresh___ water.
10. This book ___includes___ a table of contents and a map.

C Vocabulary Review: Definitions

Match the words with their meaning. Write the letter of the definition from the second column in the correct blank.

___e___ 1. hemisphere   ✓ a. not fight
___g___ 2. border   ✓ b. study
___i___ 3. remain   ✓ c. at last
___a___ 4. get along   ✓ d. inside
___b___ 5. research   ✓ e. half of the earth
___d___ 6. interior   ✓ f. isolated – *одинокий?*
___c___ 7. finally   ✓ g. line between two countries
___f___ 8. remote   ✓ h. writer for magazines
___i___ 9. turn into   ✓ i. become
___h___ 10. journalist   ✓ j. stay

d True/False/Not Enough Information

*Write **T** if the sentence is true, **F** if it is false, and **NI** if there is not enough information in the text for you to decide. Change the false sentences to make them true, or explain why they are false. Do all of the **True/False** exercises in the lessons this way.*

___T___ 1. Bering left St. Petersburg ahead of Chirikov. *p-2*
___F___ 2. It took them seven years to cross Siberia because they were *line 15* traveling on <u>horseback</u>. — *flat-bottomed boats on the rivers*
___?___ 3. Vitus Bering was from St. Petersburg.
___F___ 4. Bering spent two years exploring the east coast of Siberia. *line 23-29*
___F___ *5. Bering's and Burke's expeditions were similar.
___?___ 6. Bering's men found Eskimos in Alaska.
___T___ 7. Scurvy is caused by a lack of vitamin C.
___?___ 8. Alaska belonged to the United States at the time of Bering's expedition.

Lesson 3: Vitus Bering: Across Siberia to North America

Comprehension Questions

Paraphrase your answers. This means that you should answer the questions in your own words instead of using the exact words from the text.

1. Why was Bering's trip called a scientific expedition?
2. What did the men on the expedition do in Tobolsk?
3. Where did they stay longer, in Tobolsk or in Yakutsk?
*4. Why did the expedition have to build boats? *yo*
5. How did the two ships lose contact in the Pacific Ocean?
6. Why did the men on the island continue to die even when they had food and water?
*7. Is scurvy a problem on ships today? Why or why not?
*8. When Bering's expedition returned to St. Petersburg, were they welcomed as national heroes? Why or why not?

 Main Idea

What is the main idea of paragraph 3 (lines 14–19)?

a. It took seven years to cross Siberia.
b. The expedition explored two rivers.
c. The expedition built their own village in Yakutsk.

 Reading

How carefully should you read something? How fast should you read? The answer depends on what you are reading. Sometimes you need to read things slowly and carefully. At other times, you can read quickly, and at still other times, you can read at an average speed.

How would you read each thing below? Check (✓) the box for slowly and carefully, at an average speed, or quickly.

	Slowly and Carefully	At an Average Speed	Quickly
1. A letter from your parents	☐	☐	☒
2. A letter from your bank	☒	☐	☐

	Slowly and Carefully	At an Average Speed	Quickly
3. The textbook for a difficult science class	☒	☐	☐
4. An exciting mystery story	☐	☐	☒
5. The directions on an important exam	☐	☒	☐
6. A magazine article about an interesting person	☐	☐	☒

Some students like to read the whole text quickly to get the general idea. Others like to start at the beginning and read each sentence carefully. You can choose the best way for you to start reading a lesson. After that, you probably need to read the lesson two or three more times. When you come to a word you don't know, read the sentence again or even three times, to help you remember the word. It is never necessary to memorize sentences or paragraphs. That is not the way to study reading.

If the text is very difficult for you, read the first paragraph two or three times, then the second, and so on. Then read the whole text from beginning to end. Then you might want to read it all again.

You will probably want to read the complete text again after you have finished the whole lesson. Then test yourself on the vocabulary words that you underlined when you first read the text and learn the words you don't know.

h   Word Forms: Verbs

Every sentence must have a verb. How do you know which form of a verb to use? There are often clues that tell you what form of the verb to use.

Put the right form of the verb in each blank. Explain why you chose each form.

1. Did Bering (lead) ___*lead*___ an expedition across Siberia?
2. The expedition (leave) ___*left*___ St. Petersburg in 1733.
3. Bob is (study) ___*studying*___ about explorers.
4. Nadia has (learn) ___*learned*___ a lot of words this week.
5. Can you (help) ___*help*___ me with this exercise?
6. The teacher (give) ___*gives*___ a lot of homework every day.
7. Mr. Gordon was (sleep) ___*sleeping*___ at midnight last night.
8. They are going to (travel) ___*travel*___ in Europe next summer.

Lesson 3: Vitus Bering: Across Siberia to North America

i Prepositions

The best way to learn how to use the right preposition is by practicing. Write the prepositions in these sentences from the text.

1. _____*In*_____ 1733, the most complete scientific expedition in history __*up to*__ that time left St. Petersburg.

2. The scientists planned to report _____*on*_____ everything.

3. The expedition had to cross Siberia _____*in*_____ order _____*to*_____ reach the Pacific Ocean.

4. Vitus Bering, the leader _____*of*_____ the whole expedition, left St. Petersburg _____*with*_____ almost 600 people.

5. They traveled mostly _____*in*_____ flat-bottomed boats _____*on*_____ the rivers.

6. They had only one summer instead _____*of*_____ two years _____*for*_____ their explorations because _____*of*_____ the many problems and delays.

7. At last, the sailors _____*on*_____ Bering's ship saw mountains a short distance _____*across*_____ the sea.

8. They were _____*in*_____ a place _____*with*_____ no trees, but there were birds and animals _____*for*_____ food.

9. _____*By*_____ this time, the Russian government had lost interest _____*in*_____ the North Pacific.

10. It discovered a new part _____*of*_____ North America.

j Guided Writing

Write one of these two short compositions.

1. You are one of the men who left the island in the spring of 1742. Tell what happened to you during the decade from 1733 to 1743. Give a few details.
2. The reading does not say what happened to the people on Chirikov's ship after the two ships lost contact. What do you think happened to them?

lesson 4

Robert Scott: A Race to the South Pole

© Bettmann/CORBIS

Before You Read

1. What does this photograph tell you about the geography of the South Pole? *In South Pole is a lots of snow.*

2. What would you need in order to explore the South Pole? *food, warm clothes, dogs, ski-foot, sled pole-hand.*

3. What problems might explorers in the South Pole have? *Very cold, blizzards, no food, no water, no car,*

Context Clues

*The words in **bold** print below are from this lesson. Use context clues to guess what each word means.*

1. Robert Scott led an expedition to Antarctica for a scientific **organization** called the Royal Geographical Society.

   group of people

2. On earlier expeditions, when the dogs became **weak,** the men killed them for food.

   not strong

3. Scott had the bad luck of having **extremely** bad weather. It was often −40°C (minus 40 degrees Celsius).

   very

4. Scott and his men spent the winter near the ocean. They used sleds to carry supplies farther **inland.**

   in the land – interior

5. The men became **exhausted** and had difficulty pulling their sleds.

   very tired

4 Robert Scott: A Race to the South Pole

The first person to reach the South Pole was Roald Amundsen, a Norwegian. Robert Scott, who was English, arrived at the South Pole a month after Amundsen and died on the return journey to his ship. Yet, strangely
5 enough, Scott became a hero, but Amundsen did not.
Captain Robert Scott (1868–1912) was an officer in the English navy. From 1901 to 1904, he led an expedition to Antarctica for a British scientific **organization** called the Royal Geographical Society.
10 His group traveled farther south than anyone else had ever done. He gathered information on rocks, weather, and climate, and he made maps. When he returned to England, he was a national hero.

A few years later, Scott decided to organize another
15 expedition. He said that he wanted to make a complete
scientific study of Antarctica, but his real goal was to be
the first person at the South Pole. He took three doctors,
several scientists, and a number of other men with him.

Scott's group sailed on a ship named the *Terra Nova*
20 in June 1910. When they reached Australia, they learned
that Amundsen was also on his way to the Pole.

Amundsen and Scott were very different from each
other, and they made very different plans. Amundsen
planned everything very carefully. He took sleds and
25 dog teams, as the great Arctic explorers did. Scott took
ponies (small horses) and a few dogs, but he planned to
have his men pull the sleds themselves for most of the
trip. On earlier expeditions, as some dogs became **weak,**   **not strong**
the men killed them for food for themselves and the
30 other dogs. Amundsen did this too, and it helped him
reach the Pole, but later people called him "dog eater."
Scott would not eat his dogs, and this was one reason he
died on this expedition.

There were other differences between the two
35 expeditions. Amundsen sailed 100 kilometers closer to the
Pole than Scott did. Scott also had the bad luck of having
extremely bad weather—days of **blizzards** and strong   **storms with wind and snow**
winds. It was often −40°C (minus 40 degrees Celsius).

Scott and his men built a base camp near the ocean's
40 **edge** and spent the winter there. They used sleds and
ponies to carry a ton of supplies farther **inland** to a   **toward the interior**
place that they named the One Ton Depot. When spring
came, a few of the men started ahead of the others with
motorized sleds to leave supplies along the way.
45 However, after only a few days, the motorized sleds — *сатки*
broke down, and the men had to pull them.

A few days later, Scott started for the South Pole
with a few men. The whole journey was very difficult.
Scott and his men either walked through deep snow or
50 skied over ice and **uneven** ground. The climate was too   **not flat**
difficult for the ponies, and they all died. There were
frequent snowstorms. Sometimes the men couldn't
leave their tents for several days because of blizzards.

When Scott was 260 kilometers from the Pole, he
sent all but four men back to the base camp. This was
probably his most serious **mistake.** His tent was big
enough for only four people, and he had only enough
food and **fuel** for four. Somehow he had to **provide for**
four people plus himself. Also, one man had left his skis
behind with some of the supplies. He had to walk in the
snow, and this slowed down the whole group.

to support with money
take care of

On January 17, 1912, Scott and his men reached the
Pole, only to find a tent and the Norwegian flag. They
were not the first people to reach the South Pole. They
had lost the race.

The next day, they started the 1,300-kilometer journey
back to their base camp, pulling their heavy sleds full of
supplies. The trip back was worse than the trip to the
Pole. They became weak from hunger. **At times,** the
whiteness everywhere made them **blind.** Their fingers
and toes began to freeze, and two of the men fell and
injured themselves. They didn't have enough fuel to keep
warm in their tent. They became **exhausted** and had
more and more difficulty pulling their sleds.

sometimes

not able to see

Finally, one man died. Then another became so weak
that he knew he was **endangering** the lives of the
others. One night, he left the tent and never returned.
He walked out into the blizzard to die instead of
holding back the other three.

causing danger to

Every day, Scott described the terrible journey in his
diary. On March 21, the three remaining men were only
twenty kilometers from the One Ton Depot, but another
blizzard kept them in their tent. On March 29, they were
still unable to leave their tent. On that day, Scott wrote
his last words in his diary.

A search party found the three **bodies** eight months
later. They also found Scott's diary, excellent
photographs of the expedition, and letters to take back
to England. The search party left the frozen bodies
where they found them.

Today, the base camp building is still there. Inside
are supplies, furniture, and the men's **belongings.** They
have been left just the way they were when Scott's

expedition was there. New Zealand takes care of the
95 building and its contents.

Robert Scott's name **lives on** in stories of his trip to   continues to live
Antarctica, the last part of the Earth that people explored.
He was not the first to reach the South Pole, but he is
remembered as one of the great heroes of exploration.

a Vocabulary

organization   body   weak – sick   inland
edge   blizzard   broke down   exhausted – extremely tired
blind – not see   extremely   fuel – gaz   at times – sometimes

1. A _blizzard_ is a storm with wind and snow.
2. He put the glass too close to the _edge_ of the table, and it
   fell off.
3. A baby has more bones in her _body_ than an adult has.
   That's because many of our bones grow together as we age.
4. People who grow up near the sea are often unhappy if they have to move
   inland.
5. A _blind_ person cannot see.
6. It's very cold in northern Canada, but at the North Pole it's
   extremely cold.
7. His car _broke down_, and he had to walk five miles to get home.
8. _At times_, Burke rode horseback. At other times, he walked.
9. People need _fuel_ to cook and to heat their homes.
10. The United Nations is an important international _organization_.

Lesson 4: Robert Scott: A Race to the South Pole

b Vocabulary

weak	provided	inland	exhausted
broke down	lives on	uneven	mistake
belongings	edge	endangered	bodies

1. It was a ___mistake___ to drive into the city. There were so many cars on the road that we were an hour late for the meeting.

2. When I am traveling, I keep my ___belongings___ in a suitcase.

3. If you don't eat for several days, you will probably feel quite ___weak___.

4. When I was a child, my parents ___provided___ me with everything I needed.

5. The floor is so ___uneven___ that we can't put a table on it.

6. Ali stayed up all night to study for a test, and in the morning he was ___exhausted___.

7. She ___endangered___ her own life when she jumped off the boat.

8. A famous person's name often ___lives on___ in books and articles.

9. Is the city of Boston on the coast or ___inland___?

10. The ___edge___ of a knife is very sharp.

c Vocabulary Review: Antonyms

Match each word in the left column with its opposite in the right column.

_c_	1. remote	a. take apart
_h_	2. leave	b. exterior
_d_	3. get along	c. close to a city
_a_	4. join	d. fight
_i_	5. run away	e. together
_g_	6. include	f. having
_j_	7. uneven	g. leave out
_e_	8. separate	h. remain
_b_	9. interior	i. come back
_f_	10. lacking	j. smooth

d Multiple Choice

1. The first person to reach the South Pole was ___c___. *line 1-2*
   a. English
   b. French
   c. Norwegian *(circled)*

2. Scott was mainly interested in ___a c___.
   a. being the first person at the South Pole *(circled)* *line 10-12*
   b. collecting information about the rocks in Antarctica
   c. learning about the weather and climate in Antarctica

*3. Amundsen's expedition ate dogs because ___c___. *line 28-30*
   a. this is a custom in Norway
   b. it was a way for the men to have fresh meat *(circled)*
   c. there was no other food *(circled)*

*4. Scott's expedition had to travel ___b___.
   a. a shorter distance than Amundsen's *line 35-36*
   b. the same distance as Amundsen's
   c. farther than Amundsen's *(circled)*

*5. January is a ___a___ month in Antarctica.
   a. summer *(circled)*
   b. fall
   c. winter

6. Scott's trip to the Pole was difficult. The trip back was ___a___.
   a. more difficult *(circled)*
   b. about the same *line 68*
   c. much easier

*7. Scott and his men became exhausted because ___a___.
   a. they didn't have enough fuel and could never get warm *(circled)* *line 73-74*
   b. the sun on the snow blinded them
   c. they didn't have enough food and had to pull heavy sleds *(circled)*

8. We know the details about Scott's expedition because ___b___. *line 87*
   a. he sent reports back to the English government
   b. he kept a diary and the search party found it *(circled)*
   c. he wrote detailed letters back to England

e · Comprehension Questions

*1. Scott and Burke led expeditions in very different climates. What was similar about their expeditions? *The difficult*

2. Explain one serious mistake that Scott made.

*3. Why did Scott travel from his base camp to the Pole in January?

4. Why did one man walk out of the tent into the blizzard and not return?

5. Why was it difficult for the men to pull the sleds on the trip back from the Pole?

6. Why couldn't the three men travel the last twenty kilometers to the One Ton Depot?

*7. Was Scott a hero of exploration? Give a reason for your answer.

f · Main Idea

What is the main idea of paragraph 7 (lines 39–46)?

a. moving supplies inland
b. getting ready to ski to the South Pole
c. bad luck with motorized sleds

g · Word Forms: Nouns

There are three parts of a sentence that always have a noun (or a pronoun): the subject, the object of the verb, and the object of a preposition.

Subject	Verb	Object of the verb	Object of a preposition
David-Neel	rode	a horse	to Tibet.
The expedition	took	food	for the animals.
A storm	drove	the ship	onto an island.

The subject is usually at the beginning of a sentence. The object of the verb is usually right after the verb. It answers the question "What?" The object of a preposition comes after the preposition. There might be adjectives and other words that describe these nouns:

David-Neel rode a large black horse to Tibet.

The large scientific expedition took a lot of food for the animals.

A bad storm drove the large sailing ship onto a small island.

36

Choose a word form from line 1 of the chart to use in sentence 1, and so on. Use the right verb forms and singular or plural nouns. There are empty spaces on the chart because there are not four forms for every word.

	Verb	Noun	Adjective	Adverb
1.	include ✳	inclusion	inclusive	inclusively
2.	separate	separation	séparate ✳	separately
3.	exhaust	exhaustion ✳	exhausting	
4.	realize ✳	realization		
5.	remind	reminder ✳		
6.	inform	information ✳	(un)informative ✳	(un)informatively
7.	organize	organization ✳	organizational	organizationally
8.	weaken	weakness	weak ✳	weakly

1. Did you __include (v)__ a description of your new friend when you wrote to your family?
2. Write your two compositions on __separate (adj)__ pieces of paper.
3. He spent a long time in the desert. He suffered from heat __exhaustion (n)__.
4. After Ms. Cook got home, she __realized__ that she had forgotten to mail her letters.
5. Ms. Barber put a __reminder__ on the refrigerator for her children to do their homework.
6. Kumiko asked the teacher for __the information__ about the city buses. The teacher gave her a schedule that was very __informative__.
7. An __organization__ in Melbourne chose Burke to lead an expedition across Australia. __(no rule)__
8. He felt __weak__ before he started taking the medicine, and now the medicine has __weakened__ him even more.

Lesson 4: Robert Scott: A Race to the South Pole

h Two-Word Verbs

Learn these two-word verbs and then fill in the blanks with the right words. Use the correct verb form. Do all of the two-word verb exercises in the book this way.

run out of   =   use up; not have any more
work out   =   exercise
slow down   =   go more slowly
speed up   =   go faster
live on   =   have enough money to pay for necessities with

1. Cars have to ___slow down___ when they enter a city. When they leave the city, they can ___speed up___ again.

2. A lot of people like to go to a gymnasium and ___work out___. This exercise is good for them.

3. The Lopez family adopted two children. Now they can't ___live on___ the money Mr. Lopez gets for working.

4. Scott's men were hungry because they had almost ___run out of___ food.

i Finding the Reason

Here are some sentences about the explorers you have read about. Give a reason for each statement. The first one is done for you.

Statement	Reason
Scott and his men were cold all the time.	*They didn't have enough fuel.*
Scott went to the South Pole, because	He wanted to be the first person at South Pole.
David-Neel studied Tibetan in India. because	She wanted to go to Tibet
Bering's expedition lost a lot of its food, because	one of the ships sank in a turn
Bering took scientists with him. ,	That to explore the east cost of Siberia.
Burke died on his expedition. , because	They didn't have food.
Burke took camels on his expedition.	Because they were good for travelling and for food.
The world knows about Burke's and Scott's expeditions. because they probably	left diarries or written notes.

j Collocations – словосочетания

Some words are often used together. For example, we often use the word "join" with the word "organization."

*Read the following groups of words and then use the words printed in **bold** in the sentences below.*

join a **team**   join an **expedition**
join an **organization** join **hands**
join a **club**   join **forces** – объединиться усилий

1. Walter joined the soccer ___team___ because he is a very good player.
2. To do this dance, everyone stands in a circle and joins ___hands___.
3. If you and I join ___forces___, we'll be able to do the work more quickly.
4. I'd like to join an ___organization___ that works for peace.
5. You don't have to be a great singer to join the music ___club___.

k Guided Writing

Write one of these two short compositions.

1. You are going to lead a journey to the South Pole. What will you do differently from the way Scott did it?
2. You are in the tent with Scott in March 1912. Write a message in your diary.

lesson 5

Into the Deep:
Ocean Exploration

© Bettmann/CORBIS

Before You Read

1. Would you like to explore the ocean floor? Why or why not?

2. Would you be willing to explore the ocean in the metal ball
   shown in the picture above? Why or why not? *No, because it's very small.*

3. What are some of the dangers of ocean exploration?

   shark
   and no air
   cannot sleeps
   seas deseases
   claustrophobia (n)
   claustrophobic (adj)

   She has claustrophobia.
   I feel claustrophobic in elevators.

40

Context Clues

*The words in **bold** print below are from this lesson. Use context clues to guess what each word means.*

1. Salt water covers **roughly** 71% of the Earth.
   — almost, about

2. For centuries, people thought of the ocean as a travel **network.** It was a way to get from one place to another.

3. Sailors thought the ocean was a frightening place, full of dangerous **creatures.**
   — living things. animals, insects

4. Early diving suits allowed people to **descend** 50 feet underwater.
   — to go down

5. Scientists discovered underwater mountains and more than 4,000 new **species.**
   — kinds of plants or animals

5   Into the Deep: Ocean Exploration

Salt water covers **roughly** 71% of the Earth's **surface,** and yet we have spent much more time exploring the Earth's mountains, forests, and deserts than studying its oceans. Scientists say that we know more about the
5 moon than we know about our own oceans. And today, we continue to spend more money on space exploration than on ocean exploration.

Why is it that we know so little about the oceans that surround us? Perhaps it is because, for centuries, people
10 thought of the ocean as just a travel **network.** It was a way to get from one place to another. Most ocean travelers stayed close to the coast. Their goal was not to explore the ocean but <u>rather</u> to find new trade routes for the exchange of spices and other goods.

instead; more exactly

15 To early sailors, the ocean was also a frightening place, full of dangerous **creatures.** They thought that,

deep below, the ocean was a dark and lifeless place. Believing this, people had little **incentive** to explore the ocean depths.

20   Ocean exploration was also **hampered** by the conditions below the surface. The tremendous **pressure** of the water would **crush** an unprotected diver. Water temperature on the ocean floor was not inviting either. Vents, or openings, on the ocean floor have
25 temperatures as high as 254°F (254 degrees Fahrenheit) or 123°C (123 degrees Celsius).

    To explore below the surface of the ocean, humans needed special equipment. Early diving suits from the late eighteenth century and early nineteenth century
30 were not very useful. One type **enclosed** the diver's body in a <u>**cylinder**</u>, making it difficult to move around.

cylinder

A later type of diving suit replaced the large cylinder with a heavy metal <u>**helmet**</u>. Air from above the surface traveled through a tube into the helmet. These early
35 diving suits allowed people to **descend** fifty feet below the ocean surface for about an hour.

helmet

    In 1872, the first ship equipped for ocean exploration set out on a four-year trip around the world. The ship had two laboratories, and it carried the most advanced
40 scientific equipment of the time. Scientists on the ship tested the temperature and **density** of sea water. They gathered information about ocean currents and meteorology. They discovered an underwater mountain chain and more than 4,000 new **species.** The results of
45 this expedition encouraged interest in exploring farther below the ocean surface. To do this, however, divers needed better equipment to protect them from the pressure of water.

    Two divers, Charles Beebe and Otis Barton, designed
50 one of the early submersibles for deep-sea diving. It was a large, <u>**hollow**</u>, steel ball less than five feet in <u>**diameter**</u> and weighing 5,000 pounds. A long heavy chain connected the steel ball to a ship above. In 1934, Beebe and Barton descended half a mile below the surface of the ocean in
55 their submersible. From inside the steel ball, they were able to see extraordinary creatures. This was a great

empty; with
nothing inside

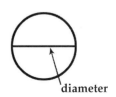

diameter

breakthrough for ocean exploration, for now people could see the underwater world with their own eyes.

60 Since Beebe and Barton's record-breaking descent, improvements have been made in diving equipment, allowing people to travel deeper for longer amounts of time. Just twenty-six years after Beebe and Barton's half-mile descent, Jacques Piccard and two others traveled to a depth of 35,797 feet, or nearly seven miles,
65 in their own much improved submersible called the *Trieste*. Even at this great depth, the explorers discovered deep-sea life and new species.

The work of deep-sea explorers has given us a picture of life far below the surface. There is now
70 greater understanding of the **diversity** of life in the ocean. We are now more aware of our dependence on healthy oceans. Still, less than one tenth of 1% of the deep ocean has been explored. Sylvia Earle, one of the leading **experts** on oceans, says, "We're in a new
75 century and a new millennium, and most of the planet has yet to be seen."

variety

Lesson 5: Into the Deep: Ocean Exploration

hamper(n) → a basket for dirty clothes

a Vocabulary

descend (to move from a higher level to a lower level) crush hollow (adj) enclosed

hamper (v), (n) expert (n) diameter helmet (n)

surface (n) (n) density (n) network diversity (adj)

1. You can drink through a straw because it's ___hollow___ inside.
2. You need to have a hard ___surface___ to write on.
3. Do you think it's easier to go up a mountain or to ___descend___ a mountain?
4. It takes many years to become an ___expert___ on something.
5. A tennis ball has a larger ___diameter___ than a golf ball.
6. If you drop a heavy weight on your foot, you might ___crush___ it.
7. The population ___density___ is higher in cities than in the country.
8. Some countries require motorcyclists to wear ___helmets___.
9. Ice can ___hamper___ a ship's movement through water.
10. ___Diversity___ is an important goal for many schools because there is much for us to learn from people who are different from us.

b Vocabulary

pressure rough rather incentive

species enclosed cylinder network

descent expert creature surface

1. There are many kinds of animal ___species___.
2. A table has a smooth ___surface___.
3. I don't need to know the exact time of your arrival. Just give me a ___rough___ time.
4. They keep their dogs ___enclosed___ in a large fenced area.
5. I'd like to go to the beach this weekend ___rather___ than the mountains.
6. Employers sometimes use money as an ___incentive___ to get people to work harder.
7. At sea level, air pushes against your body with a ___pressure___ of 14.7 pounds per square inch (1 kg per square centimeter).

44

8. Los Angeles has a huge _network_ of highways.
9. A _cylinder_ has a flat circular top and bottom and straight sides.
10. There was some kind of _creature_ living in the old building.
    We heard it, but we never saw it.

C Vocabulary Review

✓ beggar	✓ surrounded	✓ temperature	✓ civil war
✓ delayed	✓ in order to	broke down	✓ ashore
✓ decade	✓ organization	✓ details	✓ remind

1. The soldiers _surrounded_ the building so that no one could escape.
2. What does the smell of an orange _remind_ you of?
3. The snowstorm _delayed_ us for three hours because we had to drive very slowly.
4. A _beggar_ asks people for money or food.
5. OPEC is the _Organization_ of Petroleum Exporting Countries.
6. I only know she was in an accident. I don't know any of the _details_.
7. There has been a _civil war_ in Somalia for several years. Different groups of Somalis are fighting among themselves.
8. Sometimes the summer _temperature_ in Antarctica is 0°C.
9. _In order to_ get good grades, you have to do your homework.
10. A _decade_ is ten years.

d True/False/Not Enough Information

_F_ 1. More than 50% of the Earth is under water. _line 1_
_T_ 2. Early sailors were afraid to explore below the surface of the ocean.
_F_ 3. In most parts of the ocean floor, the water temperature is very hot. _line_
_T_ 4. The first diving suits were uncomfortable.
_F_ 5. The deepest parts of the ocean are lifeless. _line 66-67_
_F_ 6. Early divers carried their own air with them. _line 33_
_F_ 7. The early submersibles had motors. _line 50-54_
_T_ 8. Jacques Piccard broke Beebe and Barton's deep-sea diving record.

45

Lesson 5: Into the Deep: Ocean Exploration

Comprehension Questions

*1. Why do you think we know more about the moon than about the Earth's oceans?
 2. What hampered ocean exploration for centuries?
 3. What is an ocean vent?
*4. What was important about the 1872 scientific trip around the world?
 5. How did Charles Beebe and Otis Barton contribute to ocean exploration?
 6. How far was Jacques Piccard able to descend in the ocean?
 7. What have we learned from ocean exploration?
*8. How are the oceans important to humans?

 Main Idea

What is the main idea of paragraph 3 (lines 15–19)?

a. Early sailors didn't have a good reason to explore the oceans. _insentive_
b. Early sailors were afraid of the oceans.
c. No one knew what was in the ocean.

 Scanning

When you want to find just one detail in a text, it is not necessary to read carefully. You **scan** instead; that is, you look as quickly as possible until you find the information.

Find these answers by scanning. Write short answers (not complete sentences). Write the number of the line where you found each answer.

1. What is the temperature at vents in the ocean floor? _254°F   line 25-26_
2. What did scientists discover in 1872? _chain of the mountains line 43-44_
3. How much did Beebe's submersible weigh? _5,000 pounds   line 53_
4. What was the *Trieste*? _sibimersible   line 65-66_
5. How deep did Jacques Piccard dive? _35,797 feet (~7 miles) line 64_
6. Who is Sylvia Earle? _one of the leading experts on the ocean line 73-74_

Word Forms: Nouns

These are some common noun suffixes:

-er, -ar, -or: reminder, beggar, advisor
-ist: scientist
-ment: equipment
-ion, -sion, -tion, -ation: religion, decision, separation, realization
-y: discovery
-ity: diversity
-ness: loneliness
-ance: acceptance

Choose a word form from the chart for each sentence below. Use the right verb forms and singular or plural nouns. There are empty spaces on the chart because there are not four forms for every word.

	Verb	Noun	Adjective	Adverb
1.	trade ✳ *торговля*	trade – *торговля* trader – *торговец*		
2.	enclose	enclosure	enclosed *окруженный*	
3.	descend	descent ✳		
4.		density	dense ✳	densely
5.	diversify *разнообразить*	diversity ✳ *разнообразие*	diverse *разнообразный*	
6.	rough *делать грубее*	roughness *неровность*	rough *грубый неровный*	roughly ✳
7.	surround	surroundings	surrounded	

1. Japan and America _____ *trade* _____ with each other.
2. A lake is an _____ *enclosed* _____ body of water.
3. Beebe and Barton made a _____ *descent* _____ of half a mile.
4. Steel is a very _____ *dense* _____ material.
5. There is great _____ *diversity* _____ in the population of fish in the ocean.
6. Her father spoke _____ *roughly* _____ to her because he was angry.
7. It is not unusual for fish to _____ *surround* _____ divers. *водолазами*

Lesson 5: Into the Deep: Ocean Exploration

i Prepositions

Write the correct preposition in each blank.

1. Salt water covers roughly 71% _of_ the Earth's surface.
2. The ocean was a way to get _from_ one place to another.
3. The temperature _on_ the ocean floor varies from one place to another.
4. Diving suits _from_ the late eighteenth century were difficult to move around in.
5. Air _from_ above the surface traveled through a tube _into_ the helmet.
6. Scientists tested the density _of_ sea water.
7. A heavy chain connected the ball _to_ a ship above.
8. Even _at_ this great depth, the explorers discovered new life forms.

j Articles: The

Some geographical locations include **the** in the name.

1. Certain countries (Note that most countries do *not* include **the** in the name):

   the United States of America, *or* the United States, *or* the U.S.A., *or* the U.S.
   the United Arab Emirates
   the United Kingdom
   the Dominican Republic
   the Netherlands

2. Major points on the Earth:

   the North Pole
   the South Pole
   the equator

3. Plurals of islands, lakes, and mountains:

   the Canary Islands
   the Great Lakes
   the Himalaya Mountains

4. Oceans, seas, rivers, canals, deserts:

the Pacific Ocean
the Bering Sea
the Mississippi River
the Suez Canal
the Sahara Desert

Continents, most geographical areas, most countries, and single islands, lakes, and mountains do *not* have **the** in the name:

Asia
Western Europe (*but* the Middle East)
England
Bering Island
Lake Geneva
Mount Everest

*Write **the** in the blank if it is necessary.*

1. _The_ Panama Canal joins _the_ Atlantic Ocean and _the_ Pacific Ocean.
2. This canal used to belong to _the_ United States.
3. _____ Kuwait is near _the_ United Arab Emirates and _____ Saudi Arabia.
4. _____ Germany, _____ Belgium, and _the_ Netherlands are in _____ Europe.
5. _____ Lake Geneva is in _____ Switzerland.
6. Where are _the_ Madeira Islands?
7. _The_ Jordan is in _the_ Middle East.
8. _The_ Amazon River is in _____ South America.

k Guided Writing

Write one of these two short compositions.

1. Do you think we should spend more money on space exploration or on ocean exploration? Give reasons to support your answer.
2. You are in Charles Beebe's submersible in 1932. Describe what you see and feel while you are descending.

Video Highlights

a Before You Watch

1. Read the information in the box.

> Throughout history, explorers have gone to remote places like the North Pole to discover new things. However, you don't need to go on a long and exciting trip to explore. The word *explore* can also mean to look at something near you very closely.

2. Try it out. Explore the room around you. What do you see, hear, and smell? Copy the chart to the right and fill in the missing information at the top of the list. Then complete the list with at least three observations.

Date: _____
Time: _____
Place: _____

Observations:
The windows are
wet with rain
_____
_____
_____
_____
_____

3. Compare your list with a partner's. Did you observe some of the same things? Which things were different?

b As You Watch

Read the phrases and sentences below. They come from the video. What do you think the video is about?

1. "In the next thirty years, everything we want to find can be found."
2. "Including a 2,000-year-old Greece shipping vessel found off the coast of Cyprus."
3. "For fifty years, the Nauticos Corporation has scoured the ocean floor looking for sunken objects."
4. "Shipwrecks, marinas, even downed planes."

5. "Divers are really only good to about ten hundred feet."
6. "Worldwide, less than two companies do this kind of exploration."

Each sentence has a mistake. Watch the video and correct the sentences.

C After You Watch

1. These words come from the video. Match them to the correct definition.

   find   drop   drag   shift   identify   control

   _____ a. to pull with difficulty
   _____ b. to change from one position to another
   _____ c. to come across
   _____ d. to recognize something or someone
   _____ e. to cause to fall
   _____ f. to guide something

2. The Nauticos Corporation uses a system to find things in the ocean. Write a word from Exercise 1 to complete the sentences.

   a. _____Drop_____ sonar equipment in the ocean.
   b. _____ equipment along the sea floor.
   c. _____ target.
   d. _____ to the control room.
   e. _____ remote vehicle using joystick.
   f. _____ object.

3. Describe the system Nauticos uses to find things in the ocean. Use *first, next, then, finally.*

   Example: First, they drop sonar equipment in the ocean.

4. Discuss these questions with the class.

   a. Would you like to be a deep-sea explorer? Why or why not?
   b. If you were a deep-sea explorer, what would you like to find on the ocean floor?
   c. Do you know of any famous shipwrecks on the ocean floor?
   d. Have you or has someone you know ever found anything valuable on the beach?

Activity Page

Adventure Trail

You and your partner are two explorers who are going to travel all over the world. Like all great explorers, you will describe the different places you travel to. You will need a coin and two counters.

Put your counters on the Home square. Each person takes a turn tossing the coin. If the coin you toss lands heads up, move your counter forward one square. If it lands tails up, move your counter forward two squares. If your counter lands on a picture, describe the new place using the vocabulary words you know. Also, write two sentences about the place. Continue to toss the coin and move your counter until you reach the end (the Well Done! square). When you have reached the end, share your sentences with the class.

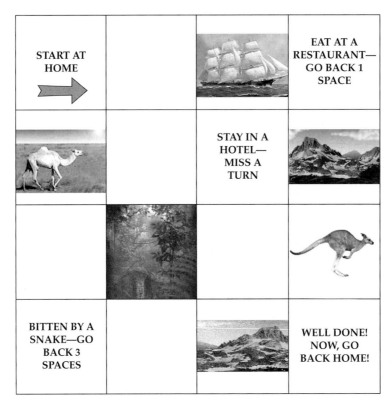

Understanding Definitions

1. Draw lines to match the following two-word verbs with their meanings.

   a. get along   return
   b. run out   be careful
   c. work out   do a series of exercises
   d. give up   have a friendly relationship
   e. get back   not work at all
   f. break down   not have any left
   g. look out   not try any more; surrender

2. You can learn new two-word verbs from your dictionary. For example, these verbs all begin with *get.* Read their definitions.

   21 *phrasal v.* [T] **to get ahead:** to succeed, improve oneself: *She got a good job and is getting ahead in life.*

   26 *phrasal v. insep.* [I] **to get away (from s.o. or s.t.): a.** to escape: *The criminal got away from the police.* **b.** to go on vacation: *I got away for a week in the Caribbean.*

   30 *phrasal v. insep.* **to get behind: a.** [T] s.o. or s.t.: to support, help succeed: *Many people got behind the politician and helped her win the election.* **b.** [I] in s.t.: to be late with one's work, payments, etc.: *He got behind in his rent payments and had to leave the apartment.*

   41 *phrasal v. insep.* **to get on with s.t. or s.o.: a.** [T] s.t.: to start doing or continue with s.t., often after interruption: *Stop watching television and get on with your homework!* **b.** [I;T] s.o.: to have a friendly relationship with: *How do you get on with your boss?*

Now write in the missing part of each verb.

a. Donna is a friendly person. She gets _____ with everyone.

b. Try not to get _____ in your homework.

c. The explorers caught a rabbit for dinner, but it got

   _____.

d. Pierre is trying really hard to get _____. He's got a good job, he's just bought a house, and he is starting college next month.

e. Both of us were tired and needed a break. We finally got _____ for a week at the beach.

f. She should stop wasting time and get _____ with her work.

g. I had an idea to increase sales. My boss got _____ the idea and sales increased 20%.

Our responsibility is to protect the Earth for a million years.
—Robert Hunter, environmentalist

NASA Goddard Space Flight Center. Image by Reto Stockli.

World Population Growth

Poom население мира

© Robert Brenner/PhotoEdit

Before You Read

31.032.925

1. How many people live in your country? In your city?   2,393 mill.

2. Think about your city with twice as many people as it has now. How would things be different?

3. Do you want to have any children? How many?

Context Clues

*The words in **bold** print below are from this lesson. Use context clues to guess what each word means.*

1. In the eighteenth century, the population of the world increased **gradually.** However, in the nineteenth century, the world's population grew very rapidly.

2. By the year 2050, researchers **predict** that the population of the world will be 9.1 billion.

3. Fresh water is **crucial** for health and food production.

4. What **effect** will 3 billion more people have on the air we breathe?

5. We don't know how long the world's supply of petroleum will **last.**

1 World Population Growth

For thousands of years, the population of the world increased **gradually.** Then, in the mid-nineteenth century, the world's population started to increase rapidly. In the 100 years between 1830 and 1930, the population of the
5 world grew from 1 billion to 2 billion people. By 1960, just thirty years later, the world's population had hit 3 billion. Fifteen years later, the population reached 4 billion. Then, just eleven years later, there were 5 billion people on Earth. In 1999, we passed the 6 billion mark.
10 Today, the world's population grows by 76 million people every year. That is about 240,000 people every day. By the year 2050, researchers **predict** that the population of the world will be 9.1 billion.

Does the Earth have the **natural resources** to support this many people? Unfortunately, the answer to this question **depends on** information we don't have. For example, we don't know how people will choose to live in the future. We don't know what their **standard of living** will be. We also don't know what new **technologies** will be **available** in the future.

We do know that the Earth's natural resources are **limited.** Fresh water, for example, is **crucial** for health and food production. However, more than 97% of the water on Earth is salt water, which is **poisonous** to both people and crops. Only 3% of the water on Earth is fresh water, and three quarters of that fresh water is frozen at the North and South Poles. Today, the **demand** for fresh water is **greater** than the supply in **roughly** eighty countries around the world. By 2025, scientists predict that forty-eight countries will have **chronic** shortages of water. At present, **desalinization**, or the **removal** of salt from salt water, is not a solution to the shortage of fresh water. It takes a lot of energy to remove the salt from ocean water, and that makes the desalinization process very expensive.

The amount of land we can use to produce food is also limited. Today, roughly 11% of the land on Earth can be used for crops, while another 20% is available for raising animals. Each year, however, more of this land is lost as cities grow and roads stretch across the land. In addition, **overcultivation** has **already** damaged an amount of farmland equal to the size of the United States and Canada **combined.** It is possible to increase the amount of farmland, but only a little. Some farmland can be more productive if people start using different farming methods, but this will not increase worldwide production very much.

Clean air is another important natural resource. However, it too is **threatened** by the growing population. The **average** person today puts about 1.1 metric tons of carbon into the atmosphere each year. Most of it comes from burning fossil fuels—gasoline,

raw materials found in nature, such as trees, oil, and natural gas

the overall quality of life that people experience

long-lasting

coal, oil, wood, and natural gas. Scientists say that the
amount of carbon dioxide in the air is already 18%
55 higher than it was in 1960. What **effect** would 3 billion
more people have on the air we breathe?

   While we have many different **sources** of
commercial energy, there is a limited supply of many of
them. Today, most of the world's commercial energy
60 comes from three **nonrenewable** energy resources—
petroleum, natural gas, and coal. Three quarters of this
commercial energy is used by **developed** countries. As
the standard of living goes up in other countries, so will
the demand for energy. Some scientists predict that if
65 everyone in the world lived like an American, our fossil
fuel supply would **last** for just fifteen more years.
   Clearly, the number of people that the Earth can
support in the future will depend on many things. The
Earth may be able to support 9 billion people, but what
70 will their standard of living be? And what effect will
all these people have on the environment?

sold in the
marketplace

economically strong

a Vocabulary

gradually — *население, произношить, предсказывать*
predict
natural resources
depends on — *зависит от*

technology — *документ*
available — *доступный (n)*
limited — *ограничен. числ*
standard of living — *уровень жизни*

crucial — *решающий, критический*
demand — *требовать (v)*
chronic — *хронический*
combined — *комбин. совершеннымй*

1. There is a **limited** amount of oil in the Earth.
2. When automobiles first became **available**, very few people could buy them.
3. If you have a **chronic** problem, it never goes away.
4. Some countries are poor because they have very few **natural resources**.
5. We don't yet have the **technology** to supply the world with energy without using oil.
6. People are **gradually** learning that we must take care of the environment.
7. When there is an increase in the **demand** *(business, money)* for oil, the price usually goes up.
8. The health of the Earth **depends on** how we use its natural resources.
9. Researchers **predict** that the use of coal will increase more than 50% over the next two decades.
10. It's **crucial** for everyone to have a supply of clean water.

b Vocabulary

threat — *угроза*
already
effect
source

commercial
developing
last
nonrenewable

combine
limit
prediction
standard

1. The population is growing faster than the food supply in many **developing** countries.
2. In our town, all of the businesses are in the **commercial** district. *район*
3. Wind is a renewable resource, while oil is a **nonrenewable** resource.
4. It's only 8 p.m., but I'm **already** tired.
5. If you use the hot water slowly, it will **last** longer.
6. Overpopulation could be a **threat** to the health of the Earth.

7. Using more solar and wind energy would have a positive _____effect_____ on the environment.
8. If you __combine__ salt and water, you get salty water.
9. The __standard__ of living is higher in some countries than in others.
10. The Internet is a good __source__ of information about population growth.

C Vocabulary Review

✓ skill	✓ rather	✓ mistake	✓ blind
✓ experts	✓ supply	✓ surrounded	include
✓ exhausted	✓ civil war	✓ species	ashore

1. Mr. Rossi was __exhausted__ after driving for ten hours.
2. For my research paper, I read many books written by __experts__ on air pollution.
3. Typing is a very useful __skill__ for students. They can learn by practicing.
4. I do not use the sun to heat my house but __rather__ oil.
5. Alice injured her eyes in an accident. Now she is __blind__.
6. There was a terrible __civil war__ in Spain in the 1930s. Almost a million people died.
7. The demand for food and water is already greater than the __supply__.
8. Overpopulation is a threat to many animal __species__.
9. The children __surrounded__ their teacher, who was giving away candy.
10. Many people think it's a __mistake__ to depend on oil for our energy.

d Multiple Choice

For the rest of the book, there will be no asterisks (*) before any multiple-choice items. You will have to decide if the answer is in one of the sentences or if you have to figure it out yourself. In this exercise, use the text and the charts to answer the questions.

World's Largest Urban Areas in Population (2004)	
1. Tokyo/Yokohama, Japan	31,224,700
2. New York City, U.S.A.	30,107,600
3. Mexico City, Mexico	21,503,700
4. Seoul, South Korea	20,156,000
5. Sao Paolo, Brazil	19,090,200
6. Jakarta, Indonesia	18,206,700
7. Osaka/Kobe/Kyoto, Japan	17,608,500
8. Bombay, India	17,340,900
9. Los Angeles, U.S.A.	16,710,400
10. Cairo, Egypt	15,863,300

World's Largest Countries in Population (2004)	
1. China	1,298,847,624
2. India	1,065,070,607
3. U.S.A.	293,027,571
4. Indonesia	238,452,952
5. Brazil	184,101,109
6. Pakistan	159,196,336
7. Russia	143,782,338
8. Bangladesh	141,340,476
9. Nigeria	137,253,133
10. Japan	127,333,002

1. There were _____ as many people in the world in 1930 as there were in 1830.
   a. twice
   b. three times
   c. four times

2. Between 1960 and 2000, the population of the world _____.
   a. doubled
   b. grew three times larger
   c. increased by more than a billion people

3. About _____ of the Earth's land can be used for raising food.
   a. 11%
   b. 20%
   c. 30%

can not use again

4. The wind and the sun are _____.
   use again a. nonrenewable energy resources —
   use again b. renewable energy resources — *battery, water*
   again+ c. limited energy resources
   again

62

(handwritten top margin) medicine + hospital
military
natural resources
education
modern
high standart
of living
advanced tech-
nology
strong, stable
economy = money

(handwritten top center/right) and the
technology
to use them — Japan   China, South korea
— England + Europe   Brazil
— USA   Australia
Germany   Singapore

5. The amount of _____ in the air has increased since 1960.
   a. fossil fuels —
   b. carbon dioxide — *it goes from cars* *(b circled)*
   c. natural resources

6. The developed countries use _____ commercial energy than the developing countries.
   a. a little more
   b. two times more
   c. a lot more *(c circled)*

7. Some scientists predict that, by the year 2025, _____.
   a. the population will reach 9 billion
   b. some countries will have serious problems getting fresh water *(b circled)*
   c. 11% of our farmland will be gone

8. _____ has the urban area with the largest population.
   a. Brazil
   b. Nigeria
   c. Japan *(c circled)*

9. In _____, the population of the whole world was about the same as the population of China today.
   a. 1750
   b. 1850 *(b circled)*
   c. 1950

10. _____ has almost the same population as Cairo and Los Angeles together.
    a. Mexico City
    b. Tokyo *(b circled)*
    c. Seoul

(handwritten left margin)
developing
countries
inflation
big changes
education-cost
a lot of many
or limited
by gender
India
Malaysia
Turkey
Chile
All of Africa

e Comprehension Questions

For the rest of the book, there will be no asterisks (*) before any questions. You will have to decide if the answer is in one of the sentences or if you have to figure it out yourself. Use the text and charts to answer these questions.

1. How has the population of the world changed in the past 2000 years?
2. Why is the standard of living different in different countries?
3. Can the amount of farmland on Earth be increased?
4. Why can't we use most of the Earth's water?

5. What is a nonrenewable energy resource?
6. Why is the demand for energy increasing everywhere in the world?
7. Is it better to have a smaller population with a higher standard of living for everyone or to have a larger population with a lower standard of living?
8. How many people can the Earth support? *чуувеиних 6 иире*
9. Which European country is among the world's largest?
10. Which urban area of the world has the largest population?
11. Do you think your country has too many people? Give a reason for your answer.

f Main Idea

What is the main idea of this reading? Write it in a sentence.
Staties about world Population and natural resources

g Two-Word Verbs

Learn these two-word verbs and then fill in the blanks with the right words. Use the correct verb form.

cut down   = cut and remove (as in cut down a tree)
figure out = find (the answer)
go up   = increase
hang up   = end a telephone conversation
make up   = think of (a new story or idea)

1. Mr. Hasegawa __makes up__ funny stories to tell his children.
2. The big old tree in our front yard is dead. We have to __cut__ it __down__.
3. I can't __figure out__ the answer to this math problem.
4. When Tom finished talking to his friend on the phone, he said "Goodbye" and __hung up__.
5. When there is a shortage of something, the price usually __goes up__.

h   Irregular Verbs

Memorize these verb forms. Then put the right form of a verb in each of the blanks.

Simple	Past	Past Participle
freeze	froze	frozen
forbid	forbade	forbidden
sink	sank	sunk
shoot	shot	shot

 (forbid)

1. The law ___*forbid*___ driving over 40 kilometers an hour on side streets in the city. You can drive 60 or 75 on main streets.
2. A small sailboat hit a rock, and within an hour it had ___*sunk*___.
3. ___*Frozen*___ food is quick and easy to cook.
4. Bob went hunting and ___*shot*___ a bear.

i   Word Forms: Adjectives

Adjectives describe nouns. They are usually before the noun. They are sometimes after the verb **be.**

These are **difficult** questions.

These questions are **difficult.**

Participles are often used as adjectives. The third form of the verb is the past participle—for example, **talked** or **frozen.** The **-ing** form of the verb is the present participle—for example, **talking.**

The world is **overpopulated.**

The **growing** population is causing environmental problems.

Lesson 1: World Population Growth

Choose a word from the chart for each sentence below. Use the right verb forms and singular or plural nouns.

	Verb	Noun	Adjective	Adverb
1.	predict	prediction	predictable	predictably
2.	shorten	shortage	short	shortly
3.	depend	dependence	dependent	dependently
4.	limit	limit	limited	
5.	populate	population	populous	
6.	care	care	careful careless	carefully carelessly
7.	use	use	useful useless	usefully uselessly
8.	combine	combination	combined	

1. Anne likes to read books with a _predictable_ ending. She doesn't like surprises.
2. The secretary was _shortage_ of paper and had to order some.
3. Many countries are _depending_ on oil for fuel.
4. The speed _limit_ in my area is 30 miles per hour.
5. What is the _population_ of your country?
6. If you are _careful_ when you write your composition, you will probably get a good grade. If you write _carelessly_, you may fail.
7. A sled is _useful_ if you live in Kuwait.
8. They use a _combination_ of resources for energy in their house—the sun, oil, and wind power.

j Articles

Put an article in each blank if one is necessary.

1. For thousands of years, _the_ population of _the_ world increased gradually.
2. By _the_ year 2050, researchers predict that _the_ population of _the_ world will be 9.1 billion.
3. We don't know how _—_ people will choose to live in the future.
4. More than 97% of _the_ water on Earth is _—_ salt water.
5. Today, _the_ demand for _—_ fresh water is greater than _the_ supply.
6. It is possible to increase _the_ amount of farmland, but only _—_ little.
7. Overcultivation has already damaged an amount of farmland equal to the size of _the_ United States and _—_ Canada combined.
8. We have many different sources of _—_ commercial energy.

k Guided Writing

Write one of these two short compositions.

1. Describe what your country is doing to help the world population problem. If it isn't doing anything, what do you think it should do? Why?
2. Describe life in your city ten years from now if twice as many people live there.

Changes in the Family

lesson

2

© Jose Carillo/PhotoEdit

Before You Read

1. How many people are in your family?

2. Where do the people in your family live?

3. How is your life different from your grandparents' lives?

Context Clues

*The words in **bold** print below are from this lesson. Use context clues to guess what each word means.*

1. In some families, grandparents, parents, children, uncles, and other **relatives** all live together.

2. In some families, mothers stay at home to **take care of** the children.

3. Since 1970, there has been a 200% increase in the number of single-parent families. The number has increased **tremendously**.

4. **Industrialization** made it possible for many young people to move to the city to work in factories.

2 Changes in the Family

Barbara Todisco, 35, and her husband, Ted, 37, have two children. They live together in what is called a **nuclear** family. A nuclear family <u>consists of</u> two generations—two parents and their children.

5   Esme Tanguay, 43, lives with her daughter, Maria, 11. They live together in a single-parent family. In the United States, a quarter of American children now **grow up** in single-parent families.

Juan Diego, 45, of Miami, Florida, has two children
10   from his first marriage. His second wife, Nancy, has two children from her first marriage. Juan and Nancy also have a child together. Juan and Nancy and the five children live together in what is now called a **blended** family.

15   Carl Jacobs, 32, lives with his wife, their two children, and his wife's mother and father. They are an **extended** family. Extended families consist of more than

is made up of

one set of parents and children. The most common type
of extended family consists of a **married couple** and one
20 or more of their married children all living together
in one **household.** An extended family might also
consist of two brothers and their wives and children.
A large extended family might consist of grandparents,
parents, children, uncles, and other **relatives.**

25   For centuries, the extended family was the most
common type of family. One benefit of living in an
extended family is that there are more people to share
the work. This was especially important in societies
where mothers had to work outside the home, raising
30 crops or gathering food. In an extended family, mothers
could work outside the home while other family
members were available to **take care of** the children and
do other household **tasks.**

       In the United States, one of the biggest changes in
35 families in the last century has been a decrease in the
number of extended families. One very important
reason for this decrease was **industrialization.** The
growth of industry made it possible for many young
people to leave their families and move to the city to
40 work in factories. By the 1920s, a **majority** of children in   more than half but
the United States were no longer living in extended   not all
families. Instead, they were living in families with a
father who went to work and a mother who stayed
at home.

45   As long as a family could **afford** to have the mother   have enough money
stay at home, this type of family was able to survive.   (for something)
For many families, however, this was not **financially**
possible. As the cost of living rose in the United States,
more and more women needed to work outside the
50 home. At the same time, an **emphasis** on equality for   special importance
men and women opened the door to new job   (placed on)
opportunities for women. Before long, single-parent   chances for
families, **blended** families, and even extended families   advancement
were becoming more common.

55   Since 1970, the number of single-parent families in
the United States has increased **tremendously.** Today,
there are roughly 90 million single-parent families with

children under the age of 18. That is a 200% increase
since 1970. Nearly 99% of these single-parent families
60 are headed by women. Many **sociologists** have studied
single-parent families to find out why they are
increasing in number. The fact that it is now easier to
get a **divorce** in the United States does not fully explain
this increase. In many countries, divorce rates **stabilized**
65 in the 1980s but the number of single-parent families
continued to increase. In order to get a better
explanation for the increase in the number of single-
parent families, it is also necessary to look at why
people aren't remarrying and why there are more births
70 outside of marriage today. These two factors are
also contributing to the rise in the number of
single-parent families.
Boutros Boutros-Ghali, the former Secretary-General
of the United Nations, once said that families "are at the
75 leading edge of change and are adapting to serious
challenges, often under very demanding conditions."
The truth is that families have always had to change
and adapt, but somehow the family has
always survived.

a Vocabulary

✓ married	✓ took care of	✓ emphasized	✓ opportunities
✓ consisted of	✓ stabilized	✓ industrial	✓ industry
✓ grew up	✓ extended	✓ nuclear	sociologists

1. The _extended_ family is larger than the _nuclear_ family.
2. Her mother _took care of_ the children while she was in the hospital.
3. When his temperature finally _stabilized_ at 100°F, the doctors were able to operate.
4. Lunch _consisted of_ salad, soup, and sandwiches.
5. Mr. and Mrs. Gorder are a _married_ couple.
6. Japan is an _industrial_ nation. It has heavy and light _industry_.
7. He _grew up_ in Canada, but he spent his adult life in France.
8. Their parents _emphasized_ the importance of studying and learning, and now all of the children are professors.
9. He had so many job _opportunities_ after graduate school that he had trouble deciding what to do.

b Vocabulary

✓ divorced	afford	✓ household	✓ stable
✓ majority	✓ sociologist	✓ task	✓ opportunity
financial	✓ couple	✓ tremendous	✓ relatives

1. Maria is from Mexico, but she has several _relatives_ in California. Three of her aunts live there with their families.
2. Her brother was married for ten years before he got _divorced_.
3. There are fifty students in my sociology class. The _majority_ of students are from the United States, but there are also five international students.
4. A _sociologist_ studies how a society is organized.
5. A bank is a type of _financial_ organization.

6. The car I saw costs $10,000, but I can ___afford___ to pay only $7,000. I guess I'll have to find a cheaper car.

7. I need a ___couple___ of dollars, not just one.

8. My father grew up in a ___household___ of twelve people.

9. My least favorite household ___task___ is washing dishes.

10. In my opinion, a house with eight bedrooms is a ___tremendous___ house.

C Vocabulary Review: Definitions

Match each word with its definition.

_f_	1. blizzard		a. instead
_j_	2. inland	✓	b. living things
_a_	3. rather		c. worse
_e_	4. belongings	✓	d. stop running or working
_h_	5. remain	✓	e. things you own
_b_	6. creatures	✓	f. bad snow and wind storm
_i_	7. expert	✓	g. make a guess
_d_	8. break down	✓	h. stay in one place
_k_	9. depend on	✓	i. someone who knows a lot about a subject
_g_	10. predict	✓	j. away from the ocean
		✓	k. need
		✓	l. better than

d True/False/Not Enough Information

_F_ 1. A blended family consists of one parent. Line – 10 – 14

_T_ 2. A nuclear family is smaller than an extended family.

_F_ 3. Parents and children are from the same generation. Line 3/4

_T_ 4. The family has changed because of industrialization.

_T_ 5. A single-parent family and a blended family both have more than one generation. line 5 – 13

_F_ 6. In the 1920s, most children in the United States lived in line 40 – blended families.

? _T_ 7. The best way to raise children is in a nuclear family.

_F_ 8. There is just one reason why the number of single-parent families *line 66-72*
has increased.

_T_ 9. As countries industrialize, family size <u>decreases</u>. *Childrence*

e Comprehension Questions

1. What is a nuclear family?
2. What is a blended family?
3. What is one benefit of living in an extended family?
4. What is one effect that industrialization has had on families?
5. How are families changing in your country?

f Main Idea

What is the main idea of paragraph 5 (lines 25–33)? Write it in a sentence.

The benefits of living in an extendeel family.

g Word Forms: Adjectives

These are some common adjective suffixes: **-able, -al, -ful, -ive, -less, -like, -ous, -t, -y.**

Choose a word form from the chart for each sentence below. Use the right verb forms and singular or plural nouns.

	Verb	Noun	Adjective	Adverb
1.	socialize	society	*social	socially
2.	*industrialize	industry / industrialization	industrial	industrially
3.	marry	marriage	*marriageable	
4.	afford		affordable *	affordably
5.	control	*control	(un)controllable	(un)controllably
6.	limit	limit	*limitless / (un)limited	
7.	separate	separation	separable / (in)separable *	
8.	depend	dependence	dependable *	dependably

1. Industrialization causes serious ___social___ problems in a country.
2. Many countries (are) trying to ___industrialize___ their economies.
3. When his daughter reached a ___marriageable___ age, he sent her to live with his sister.
4. For many people, a car (is) not ___affordable___.
5. If you drive too fast, you might lose ___control___ of the car. The car will become ___uncontrollable___
6. The supply of petroleum in the Earth is not ___limitless___.
7. The two children are ___inseparable___. They start crying when they can't be together.
8. The last person who worked here was not ___dependable___. He said that he would do things, but he didn't always do them.

h Articles

Put articles in the blanks if they are necessary.

1. They live together in __a__ single-parent family.
2. In the United States, __a__ quarter of American children grow up in _____ single-parent families.
3. Juan and Nancy also have __a__ child.
4. For centuries, __the__ extended family was __the__ most common type of family.
5. In __an__ extended family, __the__ mothers could work outside __the__ home.
6. One of __the__ biggest changes in __—__ families in __the__ last century has been __a__ decrease in __the__ number of __—__ extended families.

i Summarizing

A **summary** of a paragraph gives all the important information in the paragraph. It is usually just one sentence. A summary of a complete reading text has a few sentences.

Choose the best summary sentence for each paragraph.

1. Paragraph 4 (lines 15–24)
   a. Carl Jacobs lives in an extended family that consists of his wife and children and his wife's parents.
   b. There are different kinds of extended families, but they all consist of more than one set of parents and children.
   c. Extended families consist of more than one set of parents and children.
2. Paragraph 6 (lines 34–44)
   a. One of the biggest changes in American families has been the decrease in the number of extended families.
   b. By the 1920s, most American children lived in nuclear families.
   c. The growth of industry in the United States caused a decrease in the number of extended families and an increase in the number of nuclear families.

Guided Writing

Write one of these two short compositions.

1. In your country, how are the family lives of you and your friends different from the family lives of your grandparents when they were young? Give examples.
2. Right now, do you live in a nuclear, blended, single-parent, or extended family? What do you think your family life will be like in the future? What kind of family will your children and grandchildren live in? Why do you think this?

Lesson 2: Changes in the Family

Women and Change

lesson

3

© Stone+/gettyimages

Before You Read

1. In your country, do girls and boys get the same education?

2. Who does most of the work in your house?

3. How many women work in the government of your country? What do they do?

Context Clues

*The words in **bold** print below are from this lesson. Use context clues to guess what each word means.*

1. Many reports have been **published** on the rights of women.

2. The reports have a lot of good news, but they also have some **negative** news.

3. Women do most of the **domestic** work—for example, cooking and washing clothes.

4. Women do **nearly** 66% of the world's work.

5. Many programs help women, **as well as** men, improve their standard of living.

3 Women and Change

"Women hold up half the sky." This is an old Chinese saying. However, research suggests that perhaps women do more than their share of "holding up the sky."

5   Many reports have been **published** on the conditions and rights of women **throughout** the world. Some of the news in the reports is very **positive.** For example, 90% of all countries have **official** organizations to improve the lives of women. More than

10   half of the countries have laws to protect the rights of women, and 90% of all countries have **passed** laws to give women equal pay for equal work. WHO (World Health Organization) and UNICEF (United Nations International Children's Emergency Fund) have

15   programs to improve the health of people in developing countries, **especially** women and children. Birth-control methods are now available to more than half of the women in the world. Almost half of the children in

school now are girls, a big change from the past, because in many countries education was not available to girls.

The reports also have **negative** news. Although most countries have official organizations to improve women's lives, many of these organizations don't do anything. Women make up 50% of the world's population, but they do **nearly** 66% of the world's work. They do most of the **domestic** work—for example, cooking and washing clothes. Millions of women also work outside the home. They have become 50% of the **workforce** in many countries. For this work, however, they earn about half as much as men, and, **of course**, they earn nothing for their domestic work.

Reports also show that there are still very few women in high government **positions.** In fact, only about 15% of the positions in government are held by women. In addition, more than half of the people who can't read and write are women. Being **illiterate** doesn't mean people are not intelligent. However, not being able to read and write does make it more difficult for people to change their lives.

In developing countries, where three quarters of the world's population lives, women produce more than half of the food. In Africa, 80% of all **agricultural** work is done by women. In some parts of Africa, this is a typical day for a woman. At 4:45 a.m., she gets up, washes, and eats. It takes her a half hour to walk to the **fields**, and she works there until 3:00 p.m. She collects firewood and gets home at 4:00. She spends the next hour and a half preparing food to cook. Then she collects water for another hour. From 6:30 to 8:30, she cooks. After dinner, she spends an hour washing the dishes and her children. Finally, around 9:30 p.m., she goes to bed.

There are many programs to help people improve their agricultural skills. However, for years, these programs provided money and training for men but not for women. Now this is changing. International organizations and programs are helping women, **as well as** men, improve their agricultural production.

almost

employees, staff, workers

total number of people working

naturally; clearly

jobs; places

farming

fields

Clearly, women's lives have changed in many ways.
60 Some of these changes have been positive, giving many
women legal rights and better living conditions. Ideally,
in the future, more and more women will benefit from
new opportunities, good education, and legal rights.

a Vocabulary

✓ published	official	✓ especially	✓ domestic
agriculture	✓ illiterate	✓ as well as	of course
throughout	✓ pass	✓ positive	✓ nearly

1. What book company __published__ this book?
2. I like all kinds of fruit, but I __especially__ like bananas.
3. A __domestic__ worker does a family's housework.
4. There are many programs available to help __illiterate__ people
    learn to read and write.
5. Getting a new job was the most __positive__ thing that happened
    to her last year.
6. Overpopulation affects the environment __as well as__ the standard
    of living.
7. In some countries, school students must __pass__ an exam
    before they graduate.
8. If you have $9.80, you have __nearly__ ten dollars.

b | Vocabulary

✓ official   of course   ✓ agricultural   ✓ throughout — *all off / during*
✓ negative   ✓ field   ✓ position   workforce — *all the people who work*
publish   passed   nearly   domestic

1. He wants to go to an __agricultural__ school to learn about farming.
2. Her 12-year-old son wanted to drive the car, but __of course__ she wouldn't let him.
3. They put a fence around the __field__ so that the cattle couldn't leave the farm.
4. After working at several low-paying jobs, he finally got a good __position__ at a bank.
5. The __workforce__ of a country is made up of both men and women.
6. There have been wars __throughout__ human history.
7. The child was unhappy because his teacher said something __negative__ about his writing.
8. WHO is an __official__ organization of the United Nations.

c | Vocabulary Review: Definitions

Match the words with their meaning.

__j__ 1. relative   ✓ a. a person who studies society
__k__ 2. divorced   ✓ b. become an adult
__g__ 3. population   ✓ c. small job
__c__ 4. task   ✓ d. have enough money to buy (something)
__a__ 5. sociologist   ✓ e. extremely tired
__i__ 6. majority   f. person
__b__ 7. grow up   ✓ g. number of people in an area
__d__ 8. afford   h. way
__l__ 9. descend   ✓ i. more than half
__e__ 10. exhausted   ✓ j. family member
         ✓ k. no longer married
         ✓ l. go down

d Multiple Choice

Use the text and this chart to answer the questions below.

	Percentage of Total Work Hours Put In by	
	Men	**Women**
Cuts down forests, prepares fields	95	5
Turns the soil	70	30
Plants seeds and cuttings	50	50
Hoes and weeds	30	70
Gathers crops	40	60
Carries crops home	20	80
Stores crops	20	80
Processes food crops	10	90
Sells the extra crops	40	60
Carries water and fuel	10	90
Cares for domestic animals	50	50
Hunts	90	10
Feeds and cares for the family	5	95

Source: UN Handbook on Women in Africa.

1. According to the chart, women in Africa do about _____ of the cooking.
   a. 50%
   b. 70%
   c. 90%

2. _____ of the world's countries have official organizations to improve the life of women.
   a. All but 90%
   b. Half
   c. All but 10%

3. The average woman earns _____ the average man.
   a. more than
   b. the same as
   c. less than

4. _____ in the world are literate.

   (a.) More men than women
   b. More women than men
   c. About the same number of women and men

5. In Africa, _____ of the farmwork is done by men.

   a. 80%
   b. 50%
   (c.) 20%

6. An illiterate person _____.

   a. can't think
   b. can't speak
   (c.) can't read

7. In an African village, men do about half of the _____.

   a. weeding
   (b.) planting
   c. hunting

8. In Africa, village _____ carry most of the crops, water, and fuel.

   a. men
   (b.) women
   c. children

e Comprehension Questions

1. What does the saying "Women hold up half the sky" mean?
2. How many countries have laws to protect the rights of women?
3. Why are more women than men illiterate?
4. Give a reason why some women work more hours than men.
5. What organizations have programs to improve the health of women?

f Main Idea

What is the main idea of this reading? Write one or two sentences.

g Scanning

Scan the reading to find answers to these questions. Write a short answer and the number of the line where you found the answer.

1. What percentage of jobs are held by women?
   _____nearly 66%_____

2. What percentage of positions in government are held by women?
   _____about 15%_____

3. What percentage of countries have laws about equal pay?
   _____90%_____

4. In Africa, what percentage of the farmwork do women do?
   _____80%_____

5. What percentage of women have birth-control methods available?
   _____more then 50%_____

6. What percentage of children in school are boys?
   _____nearly 50%_____

h Articles

Put articles in the blanks if they are necessary.

1. This is __an__ old Chinese saying.
2. Some of __the__ news in __the__ reports is very positive.
3. For example, 90% of all __——__ countries have __——__ official organizations to improve __the__ lives of __——__ women.
4. Almost half of __the__ children in __——__ school now are __——__ girls.
5. __——__ millions of women also work outside __the__ home.
6. More than half of __the__ people who can't read and write are __——__ women.
7. In __——__ Africa, 80% of all agricultural work is done by __——__ women.

i Word Forms

There is always a noun after an article. There might be an adjective before the noun.

Women do most of the **housework.**

An illiterate **person** cannot read or write.

Choose a word from the chart for each sentence below. Use the right verb forms and singular or plural nouns.

		Verb	Noun	Adjective	Adverb
	1.	publish	publication * publisher	published	
приличаеть здавать переносеть →	2.	pass	passage		
	3.		(il)literacy *	(il)literate	
	4.	*position	position		
	5.		agriculture	agricultural	agriculturally
	6.		official	official	officially

1. *Newsweek* is a popular _publication_.
2. The government _passed_ a law requiring equal pay for equal work. The _passages_ of this law made many people happy.
3. _Illiteracy_ is not a problem in Japan.
4. For the photograph, he _position_ himself between his two daughters.
5. Very few people work in _agriculture_ in northern Russia. It is not an _agricultural_ area.
6. My brother is a government _official_. He says you can't get into a government building without _official_ papers.

j Connecting Words

*Use the word **but** to connect a sentence from the second column with one from the first column. Use a comma before **but**. Write the new sentences on a separate piece of paper.*

1. Some of the news in the reports is positive, but (d)
2. Half of the world's children are girls, but (a)
3. Many women work outside the home, but (f.)
4. Rich countries have the fewest people, but (c)
5. It is possible to increase the amount of farmland, but (b)
6. There is enough water in the world, but (e)

✓a. Only 41% go to school.
✓b. They use the most natural resources.
✓c. It can be increased only a little.
✓d. Some of it is bad.
✓e. Most of it is salt water.
✓f. Their husbands don't help them with the housework.

k Guided Writing

Write one of these two short compositions.

1. Is it easy to change the life of women in a society? Give reasons for your answer.
2. In your country, is the life of a young woman today different from the lives of young women fifty years ago? Give examples.

Rain Forests

TED MEAD/Peter Arnold, Inc.

Before You Read

1. Do you have forests in your country? Describe them.

2. Compare the number of trees in your country today with the number of trees there 100 years ago. Do you think there are more trees, fewer trees, or about the same number?

3. What do you already know about tropical rain forests?

Context Clues

*The words in **bold** print below are from this lesson. Use context clues to guess what each word means.*

1. People cut down a quarter of the trees to make fields for their cattle. They cut down the **remaining** trees for fuel or to sell the wood or to start farms.

2. The world needs more food, and it seems like a good idea to **clear** the rain forests and use the land for agriculture.

3. One **surprising** thing about rain forests is that the land under them is not very good. Most people think it is, but it isn't.

4   Rain Forests

Tropical rain forests are found in the Amazon **region** area of South America, as well as in Central America, Africa, and Asia. Almost half of the rain forests are in Brazil. Tropical rain forests are very old, thick forests where it
5 rains more than 1.8 meters per year. The oldest rain forest in the world is in Sarawak. It is 10 million years old, and it has 2,500 different kinds of trees.

In rain forests, there are huge trees forty-five meters high. The lowest **branches** of the trees are about ten
10 meters above the ground. Below the trees, there is another **level** of plants that consists of many kinds of smaller trees, shrubs, and flowers.

leaves
branches
roots

Each level of the rain forest is its own world. The lower level is protected by the trees above. The
15 temperature and **humidity** (the amount of water, or measurement **moisture**, in the air) stay about the same in the lower level. There is not much sunlight. In the upper level, the sun, rain, and wind change the temperature and humidity often.
20 An amazing animal world lives in the upper level. There are monkeys, members of the cat family, birds,

and insects **such as** bees, butterflies, and many kinds of
flies. Other animals that usually live on the ground also
live here—mice, ants, and even earthworms.

25 This upper level of the forest is thick with plant life
because the trees are covered with other plants. Most
plants get **nutrients** from the ground **through** their
roots. These plants in the upper level take their
nutrients from the trees they live on and from the other
30 plants that die there.

The animals in the rain forest need "streets" so that
they can move along the upper level without going
down to the ground. They make **paths** along the
branches of the trees. A researcher found a path that
35 stretched for eighteen meters in one tree. One kind of
tiny ant makes a path only three millimeters wide.

Unfortunately, humans are still destroying the
Earth's tropical rain forests. Nearly 80,000 square
kilometers are being destroyed every year. About a
40 quarter of the **destruction** comes from people cutting
down trees for fuel. Another quarter is to make
grassland for their cattle. The **remaining** trees are cut
down to sell the wood or to start farms.

The population in cities all over the world is
45 growing, and more and more wood is needed to build
huge new buildings. For example, 5,000 trees from the
Sarawak rain forest in Malaysia were used to build just
one tall building. If people continue cutting down that
many trees in the Sarawak rain forest, all the trees could
50 be gone in eight years.

The world needs more food, and it seems like a good
idea to **clear** the rain forests and use the land for
agriculture. Many people think that the land under
these huge, thick forests must be very rich in nutrients,
55 but it isn't. This is another **surprising** thing about
rain forests.

Most of the land in tropical rain forests is very poor.
The plants are able to live because of all the dead **leaves**
and other plant parts that fall to the ground. This **carpet**
60 of dead plants provides nutrients for the living plants.
When the land is cleared for agriculture, there are

for example

food

narrow ways
for walking

floor covering

no longer any plants to die and provide nutrients for
living plants. The cycle is broken. Agriculture is
unsuccessful because the land cannot support it. Trees

65 cannot grow again because the carpet of dead plants is
gone. The land becomes **empty** and useless.

not any more

Why should it **matter** to a businessperson, a farmer,
or a student that people are destroying rain forests
thousands of kilometers away? For anyone who takes

70 medicine, wears running shoes, or uses envelopes, the
destruction of the rain forest does matter. Rain forests
cover less than 6% of the Earth's area, but they have
100,000 kinds of plants, probably half of all the kinds
of plants on the Earth. Three fourths of all known kinds

75 of plants and animals call the rain forest their home.
Twenty percent of our different kinds of medicine come
from rain forests. The glue on an envelope and in shoes
comes from tropical plants. Rain forests provide
materials for hundreds of other products.

80 Rain forests are also very important to the world's
climate. The Amazon rain forest alone receives about 30
to 40% of the total rainfall on the Earth and produces
about the same percentage of the world's **oxygen.** Many
scientists believe that the decreasing size of rain forests

85 will affect the climate on the Earth, making it
uncomfortable or even dangerous for life.

The destruction of our rain forests is an international
problem. One country—or even a few countries—cannot
solve the problem alone. The nations of the world must

90 work together to find a solution before it is too late.

a   Vocabulary

✓ through	✓ path	✓ branch	such as
destruction	✓ region	✓ no longer	✓ nutrients
✓ humidity	✓ remain	✓ level	✓ roots

1. The northern __region__ of Canada is very cold.

2. He plans to __remain__ in Brazil for several years and then return to England.

3. When students do well in their English classes, they move up to the next __level__.

4. Masako left the university to go back to Japan. She will __no longer__ study English in an American classroom.

5. The __roots__ of most plants are below the ground.

6. Anne and Ken like to walk on a __path__ along the river in the evening.

7. A __branch__ is part of a tree.

8. All living things need __nutrients__ to live.

9. If you want to get to Canada from Mexico, you have to go __through__ the United States.

10. The temperature and the __humidity__ are both high in Malaysia.

b   Vocabulary

✓ cleared	surprise	nutrients	path
✓ successful	✓ matter	moisture	✓ destruction
✓ oxygen (O)	✓ such as	✓ carpet	✓ leaves

1. After dinner, they __cleared__ the dishes from the table.

2. The living room has a wood floor, but the bedroom has a __carpet__.

3. The __destruction__ of the rain forests should be a <u>concern</u>—Беспокойство for everyone.

4. It doesn't __matter__ to me if we stay at home or go to a movie.

5. __Oxygen__ is necessary for life.
6. People in Latin American countries __such as__ Ecuador, Peru, and Venezuela speak Spanish.
7. In cold climates, trees drop their __leaves__ in the winter.
8. He's a __successful__ businessperson because he works very hard.
9. It was a __surprise__ to see him at the party because he rarely goes out.
10. The amount of __moisture__ in the air is called humidity.

C Vocabulary Review: Synonyms

Match the words that mean the same.

__b__ 1. gradually   ✓ a. very
__c__ 2. nearly   ✓ b. slowly
__f__ 3. such as   ✓ c. almost
__a__ 4. extremely   ✓ d. not old
__j__ 5. enclose   ✓ e. about
__g__ 6. surprising   ✓ f. for example
__d__ 7. fresh   ✓ g. unexpected – неожиданние?
__h__ 8. turn into   ✓ h. become
__i__ 9. humid   ✓ i. moist – влажние?
__e__ 10. roughly   ✓ j. surround

d True/False/Not Enough Information

__NI__ 1. Some rain forests are not in the tropics. ℓ – 1– 4
__T__ 2. There is more change in weather in the upper level of a rain forest than in the lower level.
__T__ 3. In the upper level, some plants support the life of other plants.
__F__ 4. Plants get nutrients through their branches. ℓ – 26–29
__T__ 5. People destroy about 20,000 square kilometers of tropical rain forest every year so that they can burn the wood.

_F_ 6. The land in tropical rain forests is rich. *ℓ 57*

_T_ 7. Tropical rain forest land can support forests although it cannot support agriculture.

_Ni_ 8. Material from rain forests is used to make cassette tapes.
reproduce
_T_ 9. Earthworms make paths on the branches of trees in rain forests. *ℓ 23-24*

_T_ 10. There are rain forests in Brazil.

_T_ 11. Rain forests have 100,000 kinds of plants.

e Comprehension Questions

1. How is the weather in the lower level of a rain forest different from the weather in the upper level?
2. Why is it amazing to find mice and earthworms in the upper level?
3. Where do most plants in the upper level get their nutrients?
4. Why do people cut down trees in rain forests?
5. Where do plants in the lower level get their nutrients?
6. What happens to the land when the trees are cut down?
7. Why are rain forests important to the world's climate?
8. What are some other reasons that rain forests are important to all of us?

f Paraphrasing

Use your own words to say the ideas found in these sentences from the text. It is not necessary to use the same number of sentences. You may use more.

1. The plants in the upper level take their nutrients from the trees they live on and from the other plants that die there.
2. When the land is cleared for agriculture, there are no longer any plants to die and provide nutrients for living plants.

1. The dead trees and plants can serve as food for the plants in the upper level.

g Main Idea

2. In clearing land no more plants and food for living plants. (no life)

1. Which sentence is the main idea of paragraph 3 (lines 13–19)?
2. Write your own sentence for the main idea of paragraph 13 (lines 87–90).

1. The changes temperature and humidity between the lower level and the upper level.

2. The serious problem in the world is the destruction of rain forests.

94

h Cause and Effect

Match the causes in the first column with the effects in the second column. Write the letter of the effect by the number of the cause.

Cause	Effect
_c_ 1. There are fewer rain forests.	✓a. The weather doesn't change much in the lower level.
_e_ 2. The trees are all cut down.	✓b. They make paths along branches.
_d_ 3. A carpet of dead plants provides nutrients.	✓c. This may affect the climate on the Earth.
_b_ 4. Animals want to travel in the upper level.	✓d. Tropical plants can live on poor land.
_a_ 5. The lower level is protected by the upper level.	✓e. Tropical land becomes useless.

i Word Forms

Choose a word form from the chart for each sentence below. Use the right verb forms and singular or plural nouns.

	Verb	Noun	Adjective	Adverb
1.		tropics ✻	tropical	
2.	humidify	humidity	humid	
3.	moisten	moisture	moist ✻	
4.	empty	emptiness	empty	
5.	destroy	destruction	destructive	destructively
6.	surprise	surprise	surprising	surprisingly
7.	remain	remainder	remaining	
8.	succeed	success	successful	successfully

1. Indonesia is in the ___tropics___ .
2. It's hot and ___humid___ today.

3. It's rainy today, and my skin is ___moist___.
4. After the children left, there was an ___emptiness___ in the house.
5. War is ___destructive___. It takes human life and ___destroys___ cities, villages, and agricultural land.
6. The beauty of the forest ___surprises/d___ _-part_ me. It is a ___surprisingly___ beautiful place.
7. We ate half of the salad and put the ___remainder___ in the refrigerator.
8. She ___successfully___ flew the plane across the country. After her ___successful___ trip, her friends had a big party.

j   Noun Substitutes

Find each noun substitute in the reading. Decide what it is a substitute for. It is usually a substitute for one word, but it might be a substitute for a whole sentence.

In parts of Africa, this is a typical day for a village woman. At 4:45 a.m., **she** gets up, washes, and eats. (**She** is a substitute for **a village woman**.)

1. page 90 line 28 their _plant's roots_
2. page 90 line 29 they _plants in the upper level_
3. page 90 line 30 there _here (in the forest)_
4. page 90 line 32 they _the animals_
5. page 90 line 55 it _the land_
6. page 90 line 55 this _surprising thing about rain forest_
7. page 91 line 64 it _agreeculture_
8. page 91 line 72 they _Rain forests_

k   Articles

Put an article in each blank if it is necessary.

1. Below _____ trees, there is another level of plants.
2. Each level of _____ rain forest is its own world.
3. _____ temperature and humidity (amount of water, or moisture, in the air) stay about _____ same.

4. In _____ upper level, _____ sun, _____ rain, and wind change _____ temperature and humidity often.

5. Most plants get _____ nutrients from _____ ground through their roots.

6. These plants in _____ upper level take their nutrients from _____ trees they live on and from _____ other plants that die there.

7. _____ researcher found _____ path that stretched for _____ eighteen meters in one tree.

8. One kind of _____ tiny ant makes _____ path only three millimeters wide.

 Guided Writing

Write one of these two short compositions.

1. Why are rain forests important?

2. You are walking through a rain forest. Describe what you see, hear, smell, and touch.

lesson

5

The Garbage Project

2:30

© Francesc Muntada/CORBIS

Before You Read

1. The photograph on this page shows a landfill. Based on the photograph, how would you define a landfill?

2. Where do people in your country put old cars, old newspapers, and old clothes?

3. What do you do with food that is no longer fresh?

Context Clues

*The words in **bold** print below are from this lesson. Use context clues to guess what each word means.*

1. **Archaeologists** study buried houses, broken objects, and other old things to learn about ancient societies.

2. Students had to travel to **landfills,** where cities bury the things they don't want.

3. Many of the things we throw away, such as newspapers, glass bottles, and some metals, are **recyclables.** We shouldn't throw them away.

4. We are in **deep** trouble. If we don't do something soon, it may be too late.

5. **Hazardous** materials contain poisonous chemicals.

5 The Garbage Project

Most **archaeologists** study buried houses, broken objects, and old **garbage** to learn important things about ancient societies. At the University of Arizona in the United States, however, archaeology students are
5 **investigating** today's garbage. They hope to learn important things about **modern** society by studying its garbage. The Garbage Project started at the University of Arizona in 1973. Since then, students have studied garbage in cities in the United States, Canada,
10 and Mexico.

today's
garbage

To study the modern world's garbage, students had to travel to **landfills,** the places where cities bury their garbage. While the students were studying the garbage, they wore special clothes and used safety equipment.
15 Students were also very careful when they opened bags of garbage.

99

What have students in the Garbage Project learned from studying modern garbage? One important thing they learned is that the garbage in landfills disappears
20 very slowly. That was surprising to the students, as well as to many scientists who had predicted that roughly 70% of the garbage in landfills would disappear naturally and quickly. Even in cities where it rains a lot, the students found newspapers from 1948, forty-year-
25 old hot dogs, and lettuce from 1970.

The Garbage Project also **revealed** that what people say they do is often very different from what they **actually** do. The archaeology students asked people what they bought, ate, and drank, and then they
30 compared this to what people threw away. For some reason, the two didn't match. For example, the students found many more empty bottles of alcohol than people said they drank.

Information from the Garbage Project has also
35 helped us to see how much garbage we actually put in landfills. The students are hopeful that this will encourage us to find better ways to **dispose of** our garbage. Of course, the best way to dispose of garbage depends on what kind of garbage it is: regular garbage,
40 **hazardous** materials, or **recyclables,** such as newspapers, glass bottles, and some metals. Regular garbage goes to regular landfills. Hazardous materials, **on the other hand,** contain poisonous chemicals or metals. They shouldn't go into regular landfills.

45 Ordinary houses are full of hazardous **waste**. The most problematic hazardous waste in homes is **batteries.** When batteries **end up** in a landfill, they often break open. The poison inside them moves through rain water and other liquids to the bottom of the landfill.
50 Then it can pollute the natural water in the ground. People could avoid this problem by using **rechargeable** batteries.

Another hazardous waste from homes is motor oil. When people pour old motor oil on the ground or
55 throw it in the garbage, it poisons the environment. They should recycle old motor oil instead.

showed

really

throw away

dangerous

batteries

Unfortunately, recycling is expensive. It takes time, equipment, and special treatment. Toronto began the first recycling program in North America in 1982. The

60 city started by recycling newspapers, and later it added glass and cans to its recycling program. When students from the Garbage Project studied the Toronto landfills, they found that recycling was having a positive effect. Since 1982, Toronto has reduced the amount of garbage

65 going into its landfills by 25%.

A health official once said, "We're in **deep** trouble   serious here. We have too much garbage, our landfills are closing, and we can't open new ones because people don't want them. If we don't do something about our

70 garbage, we're going to be buried in it." The health official made that statement in 1889! Clearly, our garbage problem is not new, but as the world's population continues to grow, it will become a bigger and bigger problem.

(This article is based on an interview with Dr. William Rathje, the director of the Garbage Project at the University of Arizona.)

a Vocabulary

upsabuwsee oreosyu

dispose of	✓archaeologist	hazard	✓investigate
✓waste	✓battery	✓landfill	✓modern
✓reveals	✓actual	✓hopeful	on the other hand

1. I am not very ___hopeful___ that people will start recycling more of their garbage.
2. The hole in the street is a ___hand___ to cars.
3. That light won't work without a ___battery___.
4. I know we make a lot of garbage, but I don't know the ___actual___ amount.
5. ___Modern___ societies produce more hazardous waste than ancient societies did.
6. An ___archaeologist___ needs to have a strong interest in history.
7. Bottles, paper, and cans are examples of dry ___waste___.
8. After you cut the grass, please do not put it into a bag and take it to the ___landfill___; spread it on the garden instead.
9. It is sometimes difficult to ___dispose of___ an old automobile.
10. At the end of the movie, the hero ___reveals___ her true identity.

b Vocabulary

✓rechargeable	✓investigated	✓hazardous	✓on the other hand
✓archaeologist	✓end up	actually	✓reveal
✓recycle	✓deep	✓garbage	✓batteries

1. Don't throw that empty juice bottle away. We can ___recycle___ it.
2. They ___investigated___ the area for a week, but they couldn't find anything.
3. She didn't feel comfortable with him because he asked a lot of ___deep___ questions.
4. I could stay home tomorrow and get some work done; ___end up___, I could take the train to visit my family.
5. Putting out fires is ___hazardous___ work.

6. They said they recycled all of their newspapers, but _on the other hand_ they didn't recycle any at all.

7. The _batteries_ for my new camera are _rechargeable_. I just plug them in overnight, and in the morning they are as good as new.

8. That _garbage_ smells terrible.

9. That woman is a famous _archaeologist_. She discovered an ancient city.

10. I don't want to _reveal_ in a boring job. I hope to find an exciting job.

C Vocabulary Review: Antonyms

Match the words that mean the opposite.

_h_	1. get along	✓ a.	literate
_g_	2. remote	✓ b.	on time
_j_	3. separate	✓ c.	increase
_a_	4. illiterate	✓ d.	underpopulated
_k_	5. roughly	✓ e.	solid
_e_	6. hollow	f.	combine
_l_	7. delayed	✓ g.	nearby
_b_	8. no longer	✓ h.	fight
_m_	9. humid	i.	training
_c_	10. decrease	✓ j.	group
_d_	11. overpopulated	✓ k.	exactly
		✓ l.	still
		✓ m.	dry

d Multiple Choice

1. The Garbage Project is _____.
   a. a university program   b. a type of landfill   (c.) both a and b

2. Poisonous chemicals pollute _____.
   (a.) water   b. wastes   c. batteries

3. The Garbage Project is more than _____ years old.
   a. twenty   (b.) thirty   c. fifty

4. The first recycling program in North America was in _____.
   (a.) the United States   b. Mexico   c. Canada

5. Garbage in landfills disappears _____.
   (a.) slowly   b. completely   c. quickly

6. The most serious hazardous waste in homes is _____.
   a. newspapers   (b.) batteries   (c.) motor oil

7. The Garbage Project showed that people _____.
   a. don't know where their garbage goes
   (b.) sometimes say one thing and do something else
   c. cannot change their behavior toward garbage

8. Hazardous waste comes from _____.
   a. ordinary houses   b. factories   (c.) both a and b

e Comprehension Questions

Use the text to answer these questions.

1. Name two kinds of hazardous waste in homes.
2. Why is hazardous waste dangerous?
3. Why did students use safety equipment when they went to the landfills?
4. What is the best way to dispose of garbage?
5. What is the connection between the Garbage Project and archaeology?
6. Why did the Garbage Project go to Toronto?
7. What are three things that we can recycle?
8. Do you think the problem of disposing of garbage is serious? Give a reason for your answer.

f Main Idea

1. Write a sentence that gives the main idea for the paragraph that starts on line 17.
2. Which sentence is the main idea of the last paragraph?

g   Two-Word Verbs

✓ check in   =   tell the airline that you are there for the flight or tell the hotel that you are there for your room

✓ drop out   =   stop going (for example, to school)

✓ get through   =   finish

put back   =   put (something) where it was before or where it belongs

✓ think over   =   think about carefully

1. I can't give you my answer right away. I have to ___think___ it ___over___.
2. You have to ___check in___ at the airport forty-five minutes before your flight leaves.
3. Did you ___get through___ with your homework yet?
4. David didn't finish college. He ___dropped out___ after his second year.
5. Please ___put___ the food ___back___ in the refrigerator. Don't leave it out on the table.

h   Compound Words

Use a word from the first column and one from the second column to make a one-word or two-word compound. (More than one answer may be possible.)

___place___	1. work	✓ a. report	
___report___	2. search	✓ b. land	
___worker___	3. fire	✓ c. bag	
___bag___	4. food	✓ d. work	
___way___	5. half	✓ e. light	
___light___	6. sun	✓ f. place	
___wood___	7. house	g. production	
___work, party___	8. research	✓ h. party	
___land, place___	9. garbage	✓ i. wood	
___production, worker___	10. farm	✓ j. way	
		✓ k. worker	

i Connecting Words

*Use **and** to connect a sentence from the first column with a sentence from the second column. Use a comma before **and**. Write your answers on a separate piece of paper.*

b 1. Studying old garbage can teach us about ancient societies.

a 2. Students in the Garbage Project wear safety equipment.

d 3. We dispose of regular garbage in regular landfills.

e 4. Hazardous waste contains poisonous chemicals.

c 5. The poison inside batteries can go to the bottom of a regular landfill.

a. They open bags of garbage very carefully.

b. Studying fresh garbage can teach us about modern society.

c. It can pollute the natural water in the ground.

d. We should dispose of hazardous waste in special landfills or by recycling.

e. We must keep it out of regular landfills.

j Main Idea

What is the main idea of paragraph 6 (lines 45–52)?

The hazardous waste at home is batteries and
How the batteries can pollute the natural water

k Guided Writing

they 1) How the batteries are dangerous for enviroment.

Write one of these two short compositions.

1. Describe the Garbage Project. Tell what it is, who is in it, what they do, and why.

2. What kind of hazardous waste do we have in our homes, and how can we dispose of it?

a Before You Watch

1. In Lesson 3, you read about women in different parts of the world. Write two facts you remember about women and education.

   a. _____

   b. _____

2. Read the dictionary definition of *obey*. Do you always obey your parents? What happened when you disobeyed your parents? Discuss with a partner.

   > **obey** / oʊˈbeɪ, ə-/ *v.* [I;T] **obeyed, obeying, obeys**
   > to do what is asked or ordered: *Soldiers obey their commander's orders.*

b As You Watch

In this video you will meet a girl named Lalita. Watch the video and decide if the sentences are true or false. If the sentence is false, correct the mistake.

_____ 1. Lalita lives in Pakistan.

_____ 2. Only one in four girls goes to school where Lalita lives.

_____ 3. Lalita disobeyed her parents.

_____ 4. She went to a village school when she was 13.

_____ 5. Lalita went to a special boarding school when she was 18.

_____ 6. Lalita teaches karate now.

_____ 7. Lalita's parents are happy that she goes to school now.

After You Watch

1. What was life like for Lalita, her parents, and her village before she went to school? What is life like now? Write notes in the chart. Discuss your answers in class.

Before	After

2. Circle adjectives that you think describe Lalita. Discuss in class why you chose those words.

brave	proud	clever	shy	weak
positive	successful	modern	expert	kind
normal	strong	rude	wealthy	lonely

3. Using the words in Exercise 2, write sentences describing Lalita.

Example: Lalita is proud because she helped many girls in her village.

Crossword Puzzle

Across

3. Another word for dangerous is _____.
7. More than half of something is a _____.
8. People who study old things are called _____.
9. The opposite of *negative* is _____.
11. Your aunts, uncles, and cousins are your _____.
12. The _____ of a plant are usually under the ground.

Down

1. The opposite of *ancient* is _____.
2. A _____ pain is a long-lasting pain.
4. People who study how societies work are called _____.
5. Another word for *slowly* is _____.
6. An _____ person is someone who can't read.
10. The opposite of *full* is _____.

Dictionary Page

Working with Word Forms

1. Fill in the chart with the missing forms of each word. Write an "X" if a form does not exist. Check your dictionary if you are not sure.

Verb	Noun	Adjective
destroy	*destruction*	*destructive*
recharge		
dispose		
		surprising
	literacy	
	hazard	
	protection	

2. Your dictionary has sample sentences to help you understand differences in meaning. For example, *industrious* and *industrial* are both adjective forms of *industry*. However, they are not used in the same way. Read these sentences to understand the difference:

   Ali is wealthy because he is so *industrious*.

   Tokyo is a modern, *industrial* city.

3. Use the information on this page to help you complete these sentences.

   Example: Floods and earthquakes can cause a lot of <u>destruction</u>.

   a. Most parents will do everything they can to
      _____ their children from harm.

   b. A _____ person can read and write.

   c. _____ materials are dangerous.

   d. It is important for people to _____ of their waste in ways that will not harm the environment.

A Mishmash, or Hodgepodge

The world is so full of a number of things,
I'm sure we should all be as happy as kings.
—Robert Louis Stevenson

© Pete Saloutos/CORBIS

Roadrunners

© Joe McDonald/CORBIS

Before You Read

1. How would you describe this bird to another person?

2. Why do you think this bird is called a roadrunner?

3. What would you like to find out about this kind of bird?

Context Clues

*The words in **bold** print below are from this lesson. Use context clues to guess what each word means.*

1. Roadrunners live in the desert **zone** of the southwestern United States.

2. A roadrunner eats plants **once in a while**, but it is mostly a meat eater.

3. The bird doesn't always eat the food right there. Sometimes it **carries** the food home.

4. Most of its **diet** is insects, but it also catches birds, mice, and other small animals.

5. The male bird gives the female bird **presents** such as twigs (tiny branches of a tree) or something to eat.

1   Roadrunners

If you say the word *roadrunner* to people in the United States, they will probably think of a famous cartoon program that was on television. In the cartoon, a funny-looking bird was always outsmarting a coyote.
5 The bird in this cartoon program was based on a bird called a roadrunner.

Real roadrunners live in the desert **zone** of the southwestern United States and northern Mexico. A roadrunner is a bird, but it can fly only about as much
10 as a chicken can. People gave it its name because they usually see it running across a road, but, of course, a roadrunner spends more time among the plants of the desert than it does on roads.

The roadrunner is quite a large bird—about
15 forty-five centimeters long and twenty-five centimeters high. People laugh when it runs because it looks so funny. It holds its head **straight** out in front, and its tail

not curved or bent

113

sticks straight **out** in back. It takes long steps and can run 30 kilometers an hour.

20   A roadrunner eats an amazing variety of food. Most of its **diet** is insects, but it also catches birds, mice, and other small animals. It is even brave enough to catch tarantulas, <u>**snakes,**</u> and black widow <u>**spiders.**</u> A roadrunner eats plants **once in a while,** but it is

25 mostly a meat eater. The bird doesn't always eat the food right there. Sometimes it **carries** the food home.

snake

spider

        In the spring, a male roadrunner begins looking for a female to be his **mate.** When he finds one, he gives her

30 **presents**—snakes to eat or twigs (tiny branches of a tree) to use in building a **nest.** After they build their nest, the female lays eggs and the male and female raise their young.

        Some roadrunners become very friendly with

35 people. One couple in Arizona feeds a pair of roadrunners that come to their house every day. One at a time, each bird makes a noise outside the window. If someone doesn't immediately give the bird a piece of hamburger, the bird **knocks** on the window with its

40 beak. According to this couple, the birds behave like a pet dog or cat. For example, when the woman <u>**whistles**</u>, the birds come running. When the man leaves the house, the roadrunners walk along behind him. Clearly, roadrunners are not **shy.**

makes a sound by blowing air through the lips

45   Another couple in Arizona feeds a pair of roadrunners that come right into their house. The two birds will stand on a chair or table and watch television, and they seem really interested in what is happening on the program. In the spring, the male sometimes

50 brings gifts to the couple—an insect, or a leaf or twig for building a nest.

        In the winter, when nighttime temperatures in the desert can be 20°C colder than daytime temperatures, a roadrunner lowers its body temperature during the

55 night to save body heat. In the morning, however, the bird needs to warm up quickly so that it can run if it needs to. To warm up quickly, the roadrunner stands

114

with its back to the sun. It holds out its wings and **lifts** the feathers on its upper back. Under these
60 feathers, there is a dark **spot** on the bird's skin. This spot collects heat from the weak morning sun and quickly warms the bird's body and raises its body temperature.

Some people in Mexican villages use roadrunner
65 meat as medicine. They believe that because roadrunners can eat poisonous animals and not die, their meat should be good for human sickness.

<u>**Maybe**</u> we shouldn't laugh at the roadrunner.   perhaps
<u>**Even though**</u> it looks funny when it runs, it has   although
70 developed a special way to keep warm, and it can eat poisonous animals. It can even make friends with humans. It **fits** into its environment very well, and it doesn't matter that it looks funny.

a Vocabulary

present	diet	straight	shy
mate	knock	fit	lift
even though	snakes	maybe	whistled

1. Some _____ are dangerous, but most are not.
2. Both the female bird and her _____ take care of the young.
3. On the _____ part of the road, people drive a lot faster.
4. Tourists don't usually _____ into their surroundings because they talk and act differently than everyone else.
5. The class is going to walk to the museum _____ it is raining hard.
6. The majority of people in China live on a _____ based on rice and vegetables.
7. I thought it was a roadrunner, but _____ it wasn't.
8. John _____ for a taxi, and one stopped.
9. I can _____ the box, but I can't carry it very far.
10. When she finished college, Joan received a car from her parents as a _____.

b Vocabulary

knock	carries	spot	once in a while
spider	shy	stick out	lifts
fits	snakes	nest	zones

1. The largest _____ in the world are more than thirty feet long.

2. When I heard a _____ at the door, I went to answer it.

3. Mary watches television a lot, but she goes to the movies only _____.

4. An insect has six legs; a _____ has eight.

5. Don't _____ your tongue; it is very impolite.

6. Jean has a _____ on her new shirt, and she can't get it out.

7. The Earth has several different temperature _____.

8. He usually _____ his wallet in his pocket.

9. Birds build a _____ in the spring.

10. Even though she is very _____, she is good at making speeches.

c Vocabulary Review: Definitions

Match the words with their definitions.

_____ 1. hazardous	a. print and distribute books
_____ 2. literate	b. moisture in the air
_____ 3. landfill	c. someone who studies ancient things
_____ 4. humidity	d. someone who studies families
_____ 5. publish	e. for example
_____ 6. region	f. having nothing inside
_____ 7. archaeologist	g. able to read and write
_____ 8. recyclable	h. area
_____ 9. empty	i. very dangerous
_____ 10. such as	j. domestic
	k. a place for garbage
	l. able to be used more than once

d True/False/Not Enough Information

_____ 1. The roadrunner runs around the desert, looking for food.

_____ 2. Roadrunners live only in Mexico and the United States.

_____ 3. The female gives the male gifts in the spring.

_____ 4. A roadrunner is afraid of people and stays away from them.

_____ 5. This bird can learn to depend on people.

_____ 6. A big difference between daytime and nighttime temperatures is typical in the desert.

_____ 7. A roadrunner uses a lot of energy keeping warm in winter.

_____ 8. The roadrunner is a typical bird.

e Comprehension Questions

1. Explain why the roadrunner is not a typical bird.
2. What does a roadrunner eat?
3. Why does a male give gifts to a female?
4. Why do people laugh at the roadrunner?
5. Explain how the roadrunner gets warm in winter.
6. Do you think sick people will get better if they eat roadrunner meat? Explain your answer.
7. Do you think it is a good idea to feed wild animals? Give a reason.
8. Explain how a roadrunner fits into its environment.

f Main Idea

Many paragraphs have one sentence that gives the main idea. It can be in different places in a paragraph.

1. Which sentence is the main idea of paragraph 4 (lines 20–27)?
2. Which sentence is the main idea of paragraph 6 (lines 34–44)?
3. Which sentence is the main idea of paragraph 9 (lines 64–67)?
4. Which sentence is the main idea of paragraph 10 (lines 68–73)?

Word Forms

Nouns are often used to describe other nouns. The meaning is different than when the adjective form of the same word is used.

Cuba had a **literacy** program in the 1960s.

A **literate** person can read and write.

Choose a word form from the chart for each sentence below. Use the right verb forms and singular or plural nouns. Then circle any nouns in the sentences that describe another noun.

	Verb	Noun	Adjective	Adverb
1.		environment	environmental	environmentally
2.	complicate	complication	(un)complicated	
3.	hope	hope	hopeful hopeless	hopefully
4.	waste	waste	wasteful	wastefully
5.	dispose	disposal	disposable	
6.	depend (on)	(in)dependence	(in)dependent	(in)dependently
7.	succeed	success	successful	successfully
8.	vary	variety variation	various	
9.	finance	finances	financial	financially
10.	know	knowledge	(un)known knowledgeable	(un)knowingly knowledgeably

1. Water pollution is an _____ problem.
2. This is a _____ problem, and I can't find the solution.
3. There was a bad accident on the highway this morning. I am _____ that no one died.
4. Some _____ products from factories can be reused.

5. Doctors and dentists use _____ gloves so that they don't spread disease from one patient to another.

6. Instead of working in groups, we are supposed to work _____.

7. The movie was a huge _____, making its director a happy and rich person.

8. A supermarket sells a large _____ of products.

9. If you don't stop spending so much money, you are going to have serious _____ problems.

10. Barbara is very _____ about birds. She has been studying them for years.

h Prepositions

Put a preposition in each blank.

1. The bird _____ this cartoon program was based _____ a bird called a roadrunner.

2. Roadrunners live _____ the desert zone _____ the United States and Mexico.

3. It spends more time _____ the plants _____ the desert than it does _____ roads.

4. Once _____ a while, it eats plants.

5. _____ the spring, a male roadrunner begins looking _____ a mate.

6. Roadrunners can also become friendly _____ people.

7. The birds come one _____ a time and make a noise _____ the window.

8. The bird knocks _____ the window _____ its beak.

9. These birds come right _____ the house.

10. They seem really interested _____ what is happening _____ the program.

11. _____ the winter, nighttime temperatures _____ the desert can be 20°C colder than daytime temperatures.

12. To warm up quickly, the roadrunner stands _____ its back _____ the sun.

Connecting Words

*Use **even though** to connect a sentence from the first column with one from the second column. Write the new sentences on a separate sheet of paper.*

1. A roadrunner is considered to be a bird.
2. The Garbage Project studies landfills.
3. Rain forests cannot support agriculture.
4. We still use petroleum in cars.
5. Women do most of the domestic work.

a. They have plants.
b. It is sometimes dangerous.
c. They work outside the home too.
d. We know it pollutes the air.
e. It can't fly very far.

 Summarizing

Which sentence is the best summary?

1. Paragraph 4 (lines 20–27)
   a. It eats insects, mice, and other small animals.
   b. It eats both plants and meat.
   c. It eats a large variety of food, both plants and meat.

2. Paragraphs 6 and 7 (lines 34–51)
   a. Roadrunners follow people, ask for food, and watch television.
   b. Roadrunners can become friendly with people.
   c. Roadrunners sometimes bring gifts to people.

3. Paragraph 8 (lines 52–63)
   a. Temperatures are much colder at night than during the day.
   b. A roadrunner has an unusual way to keep warm in winter.
   c. A roadrunner collects heat from the sun through a black spot on its back.

k Guided Writing

Write one of these two short compositions.

1. Describe a roadrunner. Include the three most interesting things about a roadrunner, in your opinion.
2. Exactly how does a roadrunner fit into its environment?

Afraid to Fly

© Pierre Perrin/CORBIS SYGMA

Before You Read

1. What are some common problems airplane passengers have?

2. What makes you nervous when you are flying in an airplane?

3. Do any of these things make you nervous—standing on the roof of a building, giving a speech, snakes, or spiders?

Context Clues

*The words in **bold** print below are from this lesson. Use context clues to guess what each word means.*

1. It's smart to be afraid of some things. For example, being afraid of poisonous spiders is **logical**.

2. Some people are afraid of going through a **tunnel** on a highway.

3. A plane **crash** is always in the news, but we never hear about the millions of flights every year that are safe.

4. They listen to a tape recording of an airplane **takeoff** and landing at an airport.

2   Afraid to Fly

How do you feel about flying in an airplane? Do you find it boring, exciting, or downright <u>**terrifying**</u>?
very frightening
People who have to fly all the time for business often find it boring. People who fly only once in a while think
5 it's exciting. However, some people feel only terror when they get on an airplane. Their **fear** of flying can prevent them from traveling to other countries or visiting friends far away.

It's smart to be afraid of some things. For example,
10 being afraid of poisonous spiders is **logical.** However, if you are afraid of all spiders, even <u>**harmless**</u> ones, you
not dangerous
have an illogical fear, or a **phobia**. Three common phobias are fear of <u>**heights**</u>, fear of being enclosed in a
plural noun for *high*
small area, and fear of being in a large open area. It is
15 not logical to be afraid of these things when there is no danger, but a phobia is not logical. *крушение самолёта*

Fear of flying is another phobia. A <u>plane **crash**</u> is always in the news, but we never hear about the

millions of flights every year that are safe. Riding in a
20 car is thirty times more dangerous than flying, but most
of us are not afraid every time we get into a car. It is not
logical to be afraid of flying, but research indicates that
about 12% of people have this fear.

People with a phobia about flying are afraid for one
25 or more reasons. They might be afraid of heights.
People who have a fear of heights avoid high places,
and if they are in a high-rise building, they don't look
out the windows.

They might also be afraid of being in an enclosed
30 place like an elevator or a **tunnel** on a highway. When
they get on an airplane, they can't get out until the end
of the flight, and the flight might last several hours.

tunnel

People with a fear of flying might be afraid of the
crowds and all the noise and people rushing around at
35 an airport. This especially **bothers** older people.

Some people are afraid of the unknown. They don't
understand the technology of flying and can't believe
that a huge airplane can stay up in the air.

Others are afraid of **loss** of control. They need to
40 control every **situation** they are in. When they drive a
car, they have some chance of avoiding an **accident.** In
a plane, they have no control over anything. It terrifies
them to give up control to the pilot and the rest
of the crew.

noun for *lose*

45 For some people, a fear of flying is not important
because they don't really need to fly. But what about
someone who works for an international company?
What about an entertainer who has to sing in twenty
different places in a month? These people have to fly if
50 they want to continue in their professions.

There is help for these people. There are special
classes in which people learn how to control their fear.
They probably can't lose it, but they can learn to control
it. Then they can fly when they need to, even though
55 they probably won't enjoy it.

The class visits an airport and learns how airplane
traffic is controlled and how planes are kept in safe
condition. A pilot talks about flying through storms, the

different noises an airplane makes, and air safety **in**
60 **general.** The class learns to do relaxation exercises, and
the people talk about their fear.

Next, the class listens to tape recordings of a **takeoff**
and landing, and later the people ride in a plane on the
ground around the airport. Finally, they are ready to
65 take a short flight.

The **instructors** of these classes are sometimes   **teachers**
psychologists. They say that between 80 and 90% of the
people who take the classes are successful. They still
have their phobia, but they learn to control their fear.
70 Some of them even learn to enjoy flying.

a Vocabulary

✓ terror	✓ height	✓ fear	logical
✓ situation	✓ crash	takeoff	✓ tunnels
✓ harm	bother	✓ phobia	losses

1. A plane _____crash_____ usually kills a lot of people.
2. Tom found himself in a difficult _____situation_____, and he didn't know
   what to do.
3. A _____phobia_____ is an illogical fear of something.
4. _____Terror_____ is a very strong word for *fear*.
5. _____Fear_____ is the feeling you have when you are afraid.
6. Ali's company had so many financial _____losses_____ that it went
   out of business.
7. Some dogs bite, but most of them won't _____harm/bother_____ anyone.
8. There are several _____tunnels_____ under the rivers from Manhattan
   Island to New Jersey and the other parts of New York.
9. After _____takeoff_____, the airplane crew usually brings around
   drinks and food.
10. What is the _____height_____ of the tallest building in your city?

b Vocabulary

(handwritten in margin: Seenokouso, ganupanuun)

bother ✓	✓ accidents	✓ tunnels	✓ psychologist
✓ terrified	✓ traffic	✓ in general	harmless ✓
logical	✓ instructor	terrifying *(handwritten: ykacououeii ce)*	

1. There is a lot of ___*traffic*___ on the roads between 4 and 5 p.m., when people leave work to go home.
2. Anne was ___*terrified*___ when she saw a car coming straight at her.
3. Many more people die in car ___*accidents*___ than in plane crashes.
4. A ___*Psychologist*___ can help you learn to control your fear.
5. An ___*instructor*___ is a teacher.
6. It's raining today, but ___*in general*___ the weather here is pretty nice.
7. What is the ___*logical*___ thing to do when the telephone rings?
8. For some people, descending to the ocean floor would be a ___*terrifying*___ experience.
9. Most snakes are ___*harmless*___; only a few kinds are poisonous.
10. Please don't ___*bother*___ me now. I'm busy.

c Vocabulary Review

Cross out the word that does not belong with the other two.

1. roots, snakes, branches
2. once, couple, pair
3. knock, touch, run
4. threaten, take care of, help
5. even, even though, although
6. often, sometimes, once in a while
7. pollution, surroundings, environment
8. twenty-five, two-thirds, 40%
9. hazardous, dangerous, positive
10. married, divorced, published

d Multiple Choice

1. __b__ may think flying is boring.
   a. People who fly once in a while
   b. People who fly often
   c. People who have a phobia about flying

2. A phobia is __b__.
   a. positive
   b. illogical
   c. chemical

3. About __b__ of people are afraid to fly.
   a. 6%
   b. 12%
   c. 15%

4. A person with a fear of enclosed places doesn't like __c__.
   a. walking on a path
   b. high places
   c. being in a tunnel

5. __a__ especially bother older people.
   a. Crowds at airports
   b. High-rise buildings
   c. Spiders

6. A fear of flying is not important to some people because __b__.
   a. they are entertainers
   b. they don't need to fly
   c. they can take a class about flying

7. The instructor of a class for people who are afraid of
   flying __c__.
   a. explains about airplane crashes
   b. learns to relax
   c. takes them to an airport

8. More than __b__ of the people who take these classes are successful.
   a. 12%
   b. 80%
   c. 90%

e Comprehension Questions

1. Have you ever flown in an airplane? If you have, when was the last time you flew? *Yes, I have. Last year*
2. What are two examples of phobias? *1) fear of heights 2)*
3. Why aren't most people afraid when they get into a car?
4. Give four reasons people are afraid of flying.
5. Give four examples of people who need to fly.
6. What are three things that people learn in a class for those who are afraid of flying?
7. How does learning how airplane traffic is controlled help people who are afraid of flying?
8. Why does the class learn about the different noises a plane makes?
9. How do relaxation exercises help the people in the class?

f Main Idea

1. Which sentence is the main idea of paragraph 8 (lines 39–44)? *first*
2. Which sentence is the main idea of paragraph 11 (lines 56–61)? *last*
3. Write a sentence for the main idea of the last paragraph.
   More than 80% of the people who take the classes are successful, and they learn how to control their fear

g Word Forms: Adverbs

Adverbs describe verbs. They also describe adjectives and other adverbs. Many adverbs end in **-ly**— for example, **badly** and **nicely.** But there also are a few adjectives that end in **-ly**—for example, **friendly** and **lovely.** There are also some common adverbs that do not end in **-ly,** such as **fast** and **hard.**

Please return to the office **immediately.**

Your solution to this math problem is **completely** wrong.

Ali worked **especially** hard today.

Ann is a **friendly** person.

Mike works **hard** at his job.

Sometimes an adverb or an adverbial phrase describes the whole sentence. It is followed by a comma.

> **Most importantly,** you must hand in a report of the meeting by tomorrow morning.

> **Ordinarily,** the class finishes at 2:00. Today, it will last until 2:30 because we have a special lecture.

Choose a word form from the chart for each sentence below. Use the right verb forms and singular or plural nouns.

	Verb	Noun	Adjective	Adverb
1.		accident	accidental	accidentally
2.		profession	professional	professionally
3.	secrete	secret	secretive	secretly
4.	separate	separation	separate	separately
5.	fear	fear	fearful fearless	fearfully fearlessly
6.	lose	loss	lost	
7.	terrify	terror terrorist	terrified terrifying	terrifyingly ~~yxoreauouse~~

'much stronger than fear

1. During lunch, the waiter __accidentally__ dropped a glass of water on a customer. Even though it was an __accident__, he lost his job.
2. They did a __professional__ job on my house. No one could have done it better.
3. She took off her shoes so that she could enter the building __secretly__. She wanted her arrival to be a __secret__.
4. I don't want to ride __separately__. Let's ride together.
5. Superman is __fearless__.
6. The Student Union has a __lost__ and Found office. If you are lucky, you might find something there that you left in the cafeteria by mistake.
7. Two __terrorists__ hijacked an airplane and made the pilot fly to Paris. The passengers were __terrified__. It was a __terrifying__ experience for them.

h Articles

Put articles in the blanks if they are necessary.

1. __X__ people who have to fly all __the__ time for __X__ business often find it boring.
2. However, some people feel only __X__ terror when they get on __an__ airplane.
3. Being afraid of __X__ poisonous spiders is logical.
4. Three common __X__ phobias are fear of __X__ heights, fear of being enclosed in __a__ small area, and fear of being in __a__ large open area.
5. A plane crash is always in __the__ news, but we never hear about __the__ millions of __X__ flights every year that are safe.
6. People who have a fear of heights avoid __X__ high places, and if they are in __a__ high-rise building, they don't look out __the__ windows.
7. They might also be afraid of being in __an__ enclosed place like __an__ elevator or __a__ tunnel on __a__ highway.
8. When they get on __an__ airplane, they can't get out until __the__ end of __the__ flight, and __the__ flight might last several hours.

i Connecting Words

*Use **and, but,** or **even though** to connect a sentence in the second column with a sentence in the first column. Use a comma before **and** or **but.** Write the sentences on a separate piece of paper.*

1. Businesspeople are bored with flying, **but (d)**
2. A roadrunner fits well into its environment, **and**
3. People started exploring the ocean floor. **even though a**
4. The boat was caught in a bad storm, **and (e)**
5. Scott reached the South Pole, **but (c)**

a. **but** They didn't have good equipment.
b. It looks funny.
c. Amundsen had arrived there first.
d. People who don't fly very often find it exciting.
e. It sank.

Summarizing

Write a sentence to summarize each of these paragraphs. Number 2 will have a long sentence. For numbers 1 and 3, write a sentence with only the most important idea.

1. Paragraph 3 (lines 17–23)
2. Paragraphs 5, 6, 7, 8, and 9 (lines 29–50)
3. Paragraph 10 (lines 51–55)

 ## Guided Writing

Write one of these two short compositions.

1. Do you have a phobia? Describe it. If you wanted to control it, what would you do?
2. Describe the most terrifying trip you have ever taken, on an airplane or any other kind of transportation.

Languages and Language Diversity

bonjour

buon giorno

hello

nín hǎo

guten tag

ohaYô

gozaimasu

buenos días

© Stone/gettyimages

Before You Read

1. What languages do you speak?

2. How is your first language different from English? *Alphabet, sounds, world order.*

3. How many languages do you think there are in the world?
   ~ 6,000

Unit 3: A Mishmash, or Hodgepodge

Context Clues

*The words in **bold** print below are from this lesson. Use context clues to guess what each word means.*

1. All languages have rules for **forming** [*making*] words and for ordering those words into sentences.

2. People invent new words for their language and **borrow** [*take — брать, занять*] words from other languages.

3. Languages are now disappearing at a rapid **rate.** [*— speed*] [*predict, calculate — скорость*]

4. Experts **estimate** that the world loses a language every two weeks. [*guess, conect with math*]

5. In one study, researchers looked at **bilingual** [*able to speak 2 languages.*] adults. Some of the adults learned a second language when they were children, and some learned a second language as adults.

3 Languages and Language Diversity [*размнообразие*]

A language is a **system** of sounds, gestures, [*жесток*] or **characters** used to communicate ideas and feelings. There are roughly 6,000 languages in the world today. Some languages are used by millions of people. Others
5 have only a few speakers.

All languages have rules for **forming** words and for ordering those words into **meaningful** sentences. In written languages, meaning is expressed through a system of characters and rules for combining those
10 characters. In spoken languages, meaning is expressed through a system of sounds and rules for combining those sounds. Many hearing-impaired [*слабослышащих*] people use sign languages, in which gestures do the work of the sound system of spoken languages.

133

порядок слов

15   <u>Word order</u> is more important in English than it is in some other languages such as Russian. The sound system is very important in Chinese and in many languages spoken in West Africa.

20   Languages are always changing, but they change very slowly. People invent new words for their language, **borrow** words from other languages, and change the meanings of words as needed. For example, the English word *byte* was invented by computer **specialists** in 1959. The English word *tomato* was

25   borrowed from Nahuatl, an American Indian language spoken in Mexico. The English word *meat* once **referred** *— equal* *означается* **to** food in general.

There are several major language families in the world. The languages in each family are *родственные* related, and

30   scientists think that they came from the same parent family. Language families come in different sizes. The Austronesian family contains at least 500 languages, including Pilipino, Malay, and Maori. The Basque language, spoken in northern Spain, is the only member

35   of its language family.

The Indo-European language family contains fifty-five languages, including English. German, Spanish, Russian, and Hindi are also Indo-European languages. Another language family is Sino-Tibetan, which *китайско-тибетская бирманский*

40   includes Chinese, Burmese, and Tibetan. The *Амхарский* Afro-Asiatic family includes Arabic, Hebrew, and Amharic. There are about 150 American Indian languages spoken today. These languages have many *среди* differences <u>among</u> them and have been **<u>divided</u>** into   **separated**

45   more than fifty language families.

Today, 50% of the world's population speaks one of the top fifteen languages. The world's most common *мандаринско-китайский* language is <u>Mandarin Chinese</u>, which has more than 1 billion speakers. English is the international language

50   for science and business. In fact, English has more second-language speakers than first-language speakers.

People learn languages by listening, reading, and using the language. Most children learn their first language easily—and sometimes other languages as

Unit 3: A Mishmash, or Hodgepodge

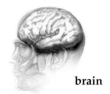

brain

able to speak two
languages

55 well. Adults often must work harder at learning a
second language. ~указывает~
Recent research ~indicates~ that a child's **brain**
actually learns a new language differently than an
adult's brain does. In one study, scientists used a special
60 machine to look at the brains of **bilingual** adults. Some
of the adults learned a second language when they were
children, and some learned a second language as adults.
The study showed that children use the same part of
their brain to learn both their first language and a
65 second language. Adults, on the other hand, used
a different area of their brain to process the
second language.
Languages have come and gone in the **past,** but they
are now disappearing at a rapid **rate.** Experts **estimate**   judge; calculate
70 that, on average, the world loses a language every two
weeks. Some **linguists** believe that half of the world's   people who study
languages could disappear in the next 100 years if we   languages
don't do anything. That would be roughly 3,000
languages lost forever. Should we let that happen?

a Vocabulary

✓ systems	characters	form	meaningful
✓ borrow	✓ specializes	✓ refer to	✓ divided
✓ past	✓ rate	estimate	✓ linguists

1. There are many different writing __systems ok__. The English
   language uses the Roman alphabet.

2. A dermatologist is a doctor who __specializes__ in problems of
   the skin.

3. The United States is __divided__ into fifty states.

4. In the __past__ fifty years, the population of the world has
   increased rapidly.

5. Can I __borrow__ your pen for just a minute?

6. It's much easier to _____form_____ wet snow into balls than to use dry snow.

7. In some countries, students _____refer to_____ — call by name their professors by their first names.

8. Noam Chomsky, a professor at MIT, is one of the most famous _____linguists_____ in the world.

9. A team of workers can build a car at a faster _____rate_____ than people working alone.

10. The word *diversity* has nine _____characters_____.

b Vocabulary

✓ rate	✓ estimate	✓ meaningful	✓ bilingual — двуязычный
✓ brain	✓ specialist	✓ reference наш	divide
past	✓ system	characters	linguistics — лингвознание

1. The best way to become __bilingual__ is to live in a foreign country. *унверпанное*

2. His friends began to worry about him when he said that there was no longer anything __meaningful__ in his life.

3. If you want to study how people learn languages, you should take a __linguistics__ course.

4. Motorcyclists wear helmets to prevent __brain__ injury in an accident.

5. I don't know the exact population of my city, but I __estimate__ that there are about 2 million people.

6. My dentist said that I need to go to a __specialist__ to get my tooth fixed.

7. During the president's speech, she made __reference__ , calling to an important new medical study.

8. The computer __system__ for the whole office was down for two days.

9. When you exercise, your heart __rate__ goes up.

10. We had such a large class that the instructor had to __divide__ it up into three groups.

c Vocabulary Review: Antonyms

Match the words that mean the opposite.

_j_	1. harmless	✓a. negative
_e_	2. instructor	✓b. full
_d_	3. once in a while	✓c. certainly
_k_	4. lift	✓d. often
_c_	5. maybe	✓e. student
_g_	6. terrify	✓f. request
_b_	7. empty	✓g. calm
_a_	8. positive	✓h. land
_f_	9. demand	✓i. fear
_h_	10. take off	j. hazardous
		✓k. drop

d True/False/Not Enough Information

_T_ 1. We don't know the exact number of languages used today.

_F_ 2. Word order is the same in all languages.   *l-15*

_T_ 3. There is more than one kind of sign language.

_T_ 4. Many hearing-impaired people use a sign language.

Nei 5. Many food words in English come from other languages.

_T_ 6. A language family can be small or large.

_F_ 7. There is nothing we can do to prevent the loss of half the world's languages.   *last parag*

_T_ 8. More people speak Chinese than any other language.   *Mandarin-Chinese*

_F_ 9. Fifty percent of the world's population speaks Chinese.   *l- 46*

_T_ 10. Adults and children use different parts of their brain to learn a second language.

Lesson 3: Languages and Language Diversity

e Comprehension Questions

1. What is the definition of a language?
2. What is a sign language?
3. In English, the basic order of words in a sentence is subject, verb, object. What is the basic order of words in your first language?
4. What is an example of a borrowed word?
5. What is an example of an invented word?
6. What is one difference between the Austronesian language family and the Indo-European language family?
7. Why is it useful to group languages into families?
8. Should we try to keep languages alive? Why or why not?
9. Why is it more difficult for adults than children to learn a second language?

f Paraphrasing

1) About 150 American Indian languages are still spoken today, and they have been divided into more than fifty languages families

Use your own words to say the ideas found in these sentences from the text. It is not necessary to use the same number of sentences. You may use more.

1. There are about 150 American Indian languages spoken today. These languages have many differences among them and have been divided into more than fifty language families.
2. Most children learn their first language easily—and sometimes other languages as well. Adults often must work harder at learning a second language.

2) There are differences in learning languages between children and adults.

g Main Idea

1. Write a sentence for the main idea for paragraph 4 (lines 19–27).
2. Write a sentence for the main idea for paragraph 7 (lines 46–51).

1) Languages are changing very slowly, and some words borrow from other languages.

2) The Mandarin-Chinese language is the most common in speaking, but English is the most common in bisnesses and science. word is language

 Scanning

1. Half of the world's population speaks one of
   the top 15 languages.
2. We might lose half of the world's languages in the next
   100 years.
3. The word *byte* entered the English language in the
   year *1959* .
4. Maori is a language in the *Austronesian* language family.

 Word Forms: Active and Passive

In an active sentence, the subject performs (does) the action:

Computer specialists invented the word *byte*.

In a passive sentence, the subject receives the action. The passive is formed with the verb **to be** and the past participle. Sometimes the person (the agent) who performed the action is included in the sentence after the word **by.** The agent is not included if it is unknown or unimportant. Sometimes everyone knows who the agent is, so naming it is not necessary.

The **word** *byte* was invented by computer specialists.

About 150 American Indian **languages** are still spoken today. (Everyone knows they are spoken by people.)

American Indian **languages** have been divided into more than fifty language families. (The people who divided the languages into families are not important in this sentence.)

Choose a word form from the chart for each blank. Use the passive form where needed.

	Verb	Noun	Adjective	Adverb
1.	instruct *одрано уши*	instruction instructor	instructive ✳	
2.		(dis)honesty ✳ *лостноси*	(dis)honest	(dis)honestly
3.	imagine *воодрзин*	imagination	(un)imaginative	(un)imaginatively
4.	invent	invention inventor	inventive	inventively
5.	interview	interview interviewer		
6.	characterize	character	(un)characteristic	(un)characteristically ✳
7.		psychology ✳ psychologist	psychological ✳	psychologically
8.	beg ✳	beggar		
9.	depend (on)	dependability	(un)dependable ✳	dependably

1. The lecture on safe driving was very _instructive_.
2. _Honesty_ is an important characteristic for someone working in a bank.
3. That mystery program was very _imaginative_. I didn't know how it was going to end until the last minute.
4. The telephone _was invented_ by Alexander Graham Bell.
5. The Minister of Health didn't like some of the questions that the _interviewer_ asked him. He _was interviewed_ by a foreign journalist.
6. Marge started a fight with her sister. This was very _uncharacteristically_ of Marge; she is usually nice to her sister.
7. Barbara is going to study _psychology_. Then she will work with people who have _psychological_ problems.
8. Dan _begged_ his friend to lend him his car.
9. Mr. Thompson is a _dependable_ person. You know that he will do what he says. You can _depend on_ him.

j Noun Substitutes

What does each noun substitute stand for?
1. page 134 line 15 **it** _word order_
2. page 134 line 19 **they** _languages_
3. page 134 line 30 **they** _languages in each family_
4. page 135 line 61 **they** _bilingual adults_
5. page 135 line 68 **they** _languages_

k Articles

Put articles in the blanks if they are necessary.
1. Some languages are used by millions of __—__ people.
2. Many hearing-impaired people use sign languages, in which __—__ gestures do the work of _the_ sound system of __—__ spoken languages.
3. Word order is more important in __—__ English than it is in some other languages such as __—__ Russian.
4. _The_ English word *byte* was invented by __—__ computer specialists in 1959.
5. _The_ English word *meat* once referred to __—__ food in general.
6. Experts estimate that, on average, the world loses _a_ language every two weeks.
7. Today, 50% of _the_ world's population speaks one of _the_ top fifteen languages.
8. Recent research indicates that _a_ child's brain learns _a_ new language differently than _an_ adult's brain does.

l   Two-Word Verbs

pick (someone) up = go somewhere (for example, with your car) to
ปีอ๊อิ้งๆ   get someone
ุภูวาน√ stand for = be a symbol for (as in *U.S.* stands for *United States*)
   see (someone) off = go with someone to the place from which he or she is
ยุ่าออ่าว   going to leave (for example, the airport)
   √ clean up = make clean and orderly (as in clean the house after a
        party or after some children had a lot of toys out)
   √ help out = help someone to do something

1. U.N. _stands for_ United Nations.
2. Tom had a big party. Afterwards, he had to _clean up_ the house.
   Three of his friends stayed to _help out_.
3. Ali studied at New York University for five years. When he left, twenty
   people went to the airport to _see_
   him _off_.
4. Let's go to the party together. I'll _pick_ you
   _up_ at 9:00.

m   Guided Writing

Write one of these two short compositions.

1. Compare your first language to the English language. How are they
   similar? How are they different?
2. What is easy about learning a second language? What is difficult?

lesson
4

Skyscrapers — небоскрёба

© Graham Tim/CORBIS SYGMA

Before You Read

1. What is the tallest building in your country? How old is it?

2. Why couldn't people build very tall buildings 100 years ago?

3. Do you think we should continue building tall buildings? Why or why not?

Context Clues

*The words in **bold** print below are from this lesson. Use context clues to guess what each word means.*

1. One of the tallest buildings in the late nineteenth century was the fourteen-**story** Pulitzer Building.

2. Cesar Pelli was the **architect** of the Petronas Towers. He worked on the building for several years.

3. A building with windows is more **pleasant** than a building without windows.

4. Architects had to find a way to prevent skyscrapers from moving too much in the wind. **In addition**, they wanted to make the buildings as beautiful as possible.

5. During World War Two, the **centers** of many cities in Europe were destroyed by bombs.

4   Skyscrapers

In 1998, the Petronas Towers in Malaysia became the tallest building in the world, **stealing** the number one spot from the Sears Tower in Chicago. Four years later, in 2003, the Taipei 101 building in Taiwan stole the **title**
5 from the Petronas Towers. It seems that no **skyscraper** can hold the title of "the world's tallest building" for very long. But how high can a skyscraper go? Some experts believe that a mile-high building (5,280 feet, or 1,609 meters) is possible with the technology we
10 now have.
    For centuries, the tallest buildings were made of stone. The base, or lower walls, of a tall building had to be very thick in order to support the upper walls. The taller the building was, the thicker the lower walls had to
15 be. One of the tallest buildings in the late nineteenth

century was the fourteen-**story** Pulitzer Building in
New York. To support the upper walls of the building,
the stone walls at the base were nine feet (three
meters) thick!

20   It took two important technological **advancements**
to make real skyscrapers possible. The first
advancement was the mass production of iron and steel.
The second was the production of lightweight metal
beams. In the 1880s, **architects** started using these
25 beams to support the walls of buildings. These
buildings didn't need thick walls at the base, so they
could be much taller.
    There were other **advantages** to building with metal
beams. The building walls were thinner, and they could
30 have more windows, which made the rooms much
more **pleasant.** With thin lower walls, there was more
room for stores and offices on the ground floor. It was
also faster to build with iron and steel than with stone.
    However, there was still one problem. How would
35 people get to the top floor of a tall building? The
solution, of course, was the elevator. Elisha Otis
invented the safety elevator and first showed it to the
public in 1853. By the 1880s, there were elevators run by
electricity, which were fast and light enough to use in
40 skyscrapers. They were developed at just the right time.
    There were other problems that architects and
engineers had to solve. They had to figure out a way to
get water to all the floors. They had to prevent the
buildings from moving too much in the wind.
45 **In addition,** they wanted to make the buildings as
beautiful as possible.
    At the same time that architects were **designing** the
first high-rise buildings, thousands of **immigrants** were
entering the United States from Europe. These people
50 needed housing, and tall buildings could provide
plenty of it in the cities. Before long, skyscrapers were
rising in cities across the United States.
    Over the years, many problems connected to
high-rise buildings were solved, and buildings got taller
55 and taller. In 1909, a fifty-**story** building was built in

floor

people who design buildings

nice

and

Lesson 4: Skyscrapers

New York, and in 1913, one with sixty floors. In 1931, the Empire State Building in New York was finished; it was 102 stories high.

60   Throughout the twentieth century, other countries were building skyscrapers too. In Europe, the **centers** of many cities had been destroyed by **bombs** during World War Two. City planners rebuilt many of the buildings **exactly** as they had been, but they also included high-rises in their plans. Most European cities today are a
65 mixture of old and modern buildings.

    Tokyo did not have tall buildings for a long time because of <u>earthquakes.</u> Then engineers figured out how to keep a high-rise standing during an earthquake. Today, there are many tall buildings in Tokyo. In fact,
70 there are tall buildings in cities throughout the world. As the population of a city increases, the number of high-rises increases because they take less **space.**

    We have the technology for skyscrapers, but do we really need them or want them? With the invention of
75 computers, a company doesn't need to have all its offices in one huge building. People can communicate by computer from offices spread out all over the city or even from their homes. And do we want 200-story buildings? Do people want to work and live that far above the
80 ground? The architects and engineers who are planning these new skyscrapers have to think about these questions, or they may build buildings that no one will use.

sudden, violent movements of the earth

a   Vocabulary

✔ skyscraper	advantages	✔ title	✔ advancement
✔ immigrants	✔ designs	✔ stories	✔ beams
✔ stole	pleasant	in addition	architect

1. Someone ____**stole**____ his car during the night. When he got up, it was gone.

2. There are many ___**advantages (n)**___ to learning a second language.

3. A high-rise building is also called a ___skyeraper___.
4. The Nile River in Africa holds the ___title___ of longest river in the world.
5. Thousands of ___immigrants___ arrive in Australia from Asia and Europe every year.
6. What was the most important scientific ___advancement___ in the twentieth century?
7. In some skyscrapers, the walls are made of steel ___beams___ and glass.
8. An architect ___designs___ buildings.
9. The Taipei 101 building has 101 ___stories___.
10. Metal beams are used to build bridges ___in addition___ to skyscrapers.

b Vocabulary

✔ pleasant	✔ immigrant	✔ bomb	✔ space
in addition	✔ architect	✔ story	✔ earthquake
advantage	✔ center	✔ exact	public

1. One ___advantage___ of steel is that it is lighter than stone.
2. We've had ___pleasant___ weather lately. It has been warm and sunny.
3. We tried to get twenty chairs into the room, but there wasn't enough ___space___.
4. An ___earthquake___ in Turkey destroyed several villages.
5. The sun is at the ___center___ of our solar system.
6. A famous ___architect___ designed the whole city of Brasilia.
7. I don't know the ___exact___ height of the Sears Tower, but I think it's more than 400 meters tall.
8. Another word for a floor of a building is ___story___.
9. The lecture on modern architecture tonight is open to the ___immigrant___. Anyone can go.
10. There was an explosion caused by a ___bomb___.

Lesson 4: Skyscrapers

c Vocabulary Review: Definitions

Match the words with the definitions.

_d_	1. estimate		a. better
_j_	2. interior	✔	b. half of the Earth
_g_	3. border	✔	c. get away from
_m_	4. delay	✔	d. guess; predict
_h_	5. blind	✔	e. not dangerous
_e_	6. harmless	✔	f. to the shore
_c_	7. escape	✔	g. line between two countries
_b_	8. hemisphere	✔	h. not able to see
_f_	9. ashore		i. remote
_l_	10. blizzard	✔	j. inside
			k. accident
		✔	l. bad winter storm
		✔	m. cause to be late

d Multiple Choice

1. The first skyscraper was built in _____.
   a. the late nineteenth century
   b. 1853
   c. Tokyo

2. It's impossible to build a skyscraper in stone because _____.
   a. the building walls would be too thin
   b. the lower walls would be too thick
   c. people couldn't get to the top of the building

3. Many European cities _____.
   a. were destroyed by earthquakes
   b. have only new buildings
   c. have both old and new buildings

4. A building with steel beams does not need _____.
   a. technology
   b. thick walls
   c. stores and offices on the first floor

5. The first building with sixty floors was built only _10_ years after a fifty-story building.
   a. 1913
   (b.) four
   c. eighteen
6. As population increases, _____ increases.
   a. immigration
   (b.) the number of skyscrapers
   c. the number of old buildings
7. There weren't any skyscrapers in Tokyo for a long time because of _____.
   (a.) earthquakes
   b. the population
   c. immigration

e Comprehension Questions

1. What technological advancements made skyscrapers possible?
2. Why don't buildings with steel beams need thick lower walls?
3. Name an advantage of buildings with thin lower walls.
4. Why does the text say that elevators were invented at just the right time?
5. What effect did the arrival of thousands of immigrants in the United States have on skyscrapers?
6. What is the tallest building in the world today?
7. What is the advantage of high-rise buildings over lower buildings?
8. Why can Japan have skyscrapers today when it couldn't before?
9. Do you think people would use 200-story buildings? What is your reason?

f Main Idea

1. Which sentence gives the main idea in paragraph 3 (lines 20–27)? First
2. Which sentence gives the main idea in paragraph 6 (lines 41–46)? First
3. Write a sentence that gives the main idea of paragraph 7 (lines 47–52).
4. Write a sentence that gives the main idea of the last paragraph.

3. Thousands of immigrants arrived to the US, after that skyscrapers rose in cities across the U.S.
4. There are many questions about building and using skyscrapers.

 Word Forms

These are some common verb prefixes and suffixes:

en-: encircle, enclose
-en: darken, shorten
-ize: industrialize, publicize

Choose a word form from the chart for each sentence below. Use the right verb forms and singular or plural nouns.

	Verb	Noun	Adjective	Adverb
1.	compare	comparison 2✳	comparative	comparatively 1✳
2.	please *справиться parobeab*	pleasure ✳ *удовольствие*	(un)pleasant	(un)pleasantly
3.	add	addition	additional	additionally ✳
4.	advance ✳ *продолжать*	advancement *продолжение*	advanced *продвинутый*	
5. *преобразовать*		(dis)advantage *преимущество*	(dis)advantageous ✳	(dis)advantageously
6. *предотвращать*	prevent	prevention *предотвращение*	preventive *предупредительный* ✳	
7.	immigrate *переселяться*	immigration immigrant	immigration ✳ immigrant	
8.	popularize	popularity ✳	popular	popularly
9. *окружать загораживать*	enclose	enclosure *ограда* ✳	enclosed	
10.	strengthen *усилить, укрепить*	strength *сила, прочность*	strong	strongly ✳

1. Spanish spelling is __comparatively__ easy to learn. By __comparison__ , English spelling is difficult.
2. It was a __pleasure__ to meet you.
3. People who are afraid to fly don't like being closed in. __Additionally__ , they sometimes fear heights and don't understand the technology of flying.
4. What can you do to __advance__ in your profession?
5. It is __advantageous__ to learn English. Are there __any__ – negative __dis advantages__ to learning it?

150

Unit 3: A Mishmash, or Hodgepodge

6. Providing _preventive_ medicine is better than helping people after they are sick.
7. The _immigration_ office is open from 9:00 to 5:00.
8. _Popularity_ is very important to teenagers.
9. The farmer put his sheep in an _enclosure_ for the night.
10. I agree with you _strongly_.

h Two-Word Verbs: Review

Put the right word in each blank.

1. There was a long line waiting to check _in_ at the airport.
2. A large truck broke _down_ on the highway.
3. Alice goes to the gym every weekend to work _out_.
4. Do you have enough money to live _on_ ?
5. Could you help me _out_ this weekend?
6. Fixing my car turned _into_ an all-day job.
7. Mr. Brown is working too hard and has to slow _down_.
8. Jean had to drop _out_ of school and get a job.
9. Children don't like to put _back_ their toys when they finish playing.
10. Bob was an hour late because he ran _away_ _from_ gas.

i Articles

Put articles in the blanks if they are needed.

1. In 1998, _the_ Petronas Towers in _—_ Malaysia became _the_ tallest building in _the_ world.
2. For centuries, _the_ tallest buildings were made of _—_ stone.
3. In _the_ 1880s, _—_ architects started using these beams to support _the_ walls of buildings.
4. Elisha Otis invented _the_ safety elevator and first showed it to _the_ public in _—_ 1853.
5. In 1931, _the_ Empire State Building in _—_ New York was finished; it was 102 stories high.
6. With _the_ invention of _—_ computers, _a_ company doesn't need to have all its offices in one huge building.

Summarizing

Write a sentence to summarize each of these paragraphs.

1. Paragraph 1 (lines 1–10)
2. Paragraph 2 (lines 11–19)
3. Paragraph 5 (lines 34–40)

 Guided Writing

Write one of these two short compositions.

1. Do you think we should continue to build higher and higher buildings? Why or why not?
2. Describe a skyscraper you have seen. Be very specific and give complete details.

Ⓙ

1). There are many skyscrapers in the world from 1998 by now, and possibility to built them higher with modern technology

2) In the past the tallest buildings were made from stone, and their lower walls were very thick.

3) The problem of getting to the top floor of a tall building was resolved by elevator.

Left-Handedness

© Jeff Greenberg/PhotoEdit

Before You Read

1. How many people in the picture are writing with their left hand?

2. Are you left-handed, or is anyone else in your family left-handed?

3. What advantages and disadvantages are there to being left-handed?

Context Clues

*The words in **bold** print are from this lesson. Use context clues to guess what each word means.*

1. Do you **prefer** to write with your left hand or your right hand?

2. In the past, left-handed people were often **forced** to use their right hand.

3. One part of the brain controls how a person uses the five **senses**—sight, hearing, smell, taste, and touch.

4. Some left-handed children see letters and words **backwards**. They read *d* for *b* and *was* for *saw*.

5. In the 1930s, some teachers started **permitting** schoolchildren to write with their left hand.

5   Left-Handedness

Do you **<u>prefer</u>** to write with your left hand? If you do, you are one of the millions of "lefties" in the world. There would be even more left-handed people in the world if many people weren't **forced** to use their
5   right hand.

     like better

    To understand left-handedness, it is **necessary** to look at the brain. The brain is divided into two hemispheres. In most right-handers, the left hemisphere is the center of language and logical thinking. This is where they do their
10   math problems and **memorize** vocabulary. The right hemisphere controls how they understand **<u>broad</u>**, general ideas and how they **respond** to the five **senses**—sight, hearing, smell, taste, and touch.

     covering many topics

    The left hemisphere of the brain controls the right
15   side of the body, and the right hemisphere controls the left side. Both sides of the body receive the same information from the brain because both hemispheres

154

are connected. However, in right-handed people, the left hemisphere is stronger. In left-handed people, it is
20 the right hemisphere that is stronger.

Different handedness causes differences in people. Although the left hemisphere controls language in most right-handers, 40% of left-handers have the language center in the right hemisphere. The other 60% use the
25 left side of the brain or both sides for language.

Lefties prefer not only the left hand but also the left foot. They prefer using the left foot to kick a ball because their whole body is "left-handed."

There has been an increasing amount of research on
30 handedness. For example, one psychologist says that left-handers are more **likely** to have good imaginations. They are also more likely than right-handers to enjoy swimming underwater. That is because left-handers can **adjust** more easily to seeing underwater.

change

35 Left-handedness can cause problems for people. Some left-handed children see letters and words **backwards.** They read *d* for *b* and *was* for *saw*. Another problem is **stuttering.** Some left-handed children start to stutter when they are forced to write with their right
40 hand. Queen Elizabeth II's father, King George VI, had to change from left- to right-handed writing when he was a child, and he stuttered all his life.

repeating words or parts of words

Anthropologists think that the earliest people were about 50% right-handed and 50% left-handed because
45 ancient **tools** from before 8000 B.C. could be used with either hand. But by 3500 B.C., the tools, which were better designed, were for use with only one hand. More than half of them were for right-handed people.

people who study different cultures

The first writing system, invented by the
50 Phoenicians (3000–2000 B.C.) in the Middle East, went from right to left. The Greeks began to write from left to right around the fifth century B.C. because they increasingly believed that right was "good" and left was "bad." As time passed, more and more customs
55 connected left with "bad." This belief is still common in many countries today, and left-handed people **suffer** because of it.

experience difficulties or pain

155

As the centuries passed and **education** spread to more levels of society, more and more people became
60 literate. As more children learned to write, more of them were forced to write with their right hand. In the 1930s, some teachers finally started **permitting** schoolchildren to write with their left hand. In some countries, however, left-handed children are still forced to write
65 with their right hand.

Many famous people were left-handed. Napoleon, Michelangelo, Beethoven, Isaac Newton, and Albert Einstein were all left-handed. Alexander the Great and Queen Victoria of England were left-handed too. Paul
70 McCartney of the Beatles plays the guitar the **opposite** way from other guitarists because he is left-handed.

Are you left-handed even though you write with your right hand? Take this test to find out. Draw a circle first with one hand and then with the other. If you draw
75 the circles **clockwise** (the direction the hands of a clock go in), you are probably left-handed. If you draw them **counterclockwise** (in the other direction), you are right-handed. The test does not always work, and some people draw one circle in one direction and the other
80 circle in the other direction. But don't worry if you are left-handed. You are **in good company.**

with a lot of other good people

a Vocabulary

✓ necessary	broader	✓ backwards	✓ stutter
✓ senses	✓ responding	force	✓ prefer
✓ memorize	tool	✓ adjust (change)	likely

1. The main streets of a city are _____ than the side streets. Broadway is a common street name.

2. A left-handed person who is forced to write with the right hand may begin to __stutter__ .

3. A car can go forward and __backwards__ .

4. Did you __*memorize*__ any poems when you were a child?

5. Do you __*prefer*__ to have coffee or tea in the morning?

6. A blind person is lacking one of the __*senses*__.

7. Some students are shy about __*responding*__ to questions in class.

8. As you drive off the highway, you need to __*adjust*__ your speed.

9. Many businesspeople agree that it's __*necessary*__ to know English today.

10. There are no clouds in the sky today, so it's not _____ to rain.

b Vocabulary

suffering	tools	force	anthropologist
broad	respond	permit	counterclockwise
education	opposite	clockwise	company

1. A mechanic cannot fix a car without _____.

2. If you want to get a good _____, where should you go to school?

3. The hands of a clock move in a _____ direction.

4. Parents should not _____ their children to swim in the pool without an adult there.

5. We had lots of _____ this weekend. My relatives and my wife's relatives all came over.

6. If you turn to the left, you are turning in a _____ direction.

7. The _____ of *north* is *south*.

8. A person who studies ancient cultures is called an _____.

9. He tried to _____ the door open, but it wouldn't move.

10. During a war, there is a tremendous amount of _____.

157

c Vocabulary Review

sticks out	borrow	mates	nests
once in a while	specialist	exactly	crash
fear	tunnel	loss	terrified

1. Do you know _____ how tall you are?
2. In spring, animals search for _____.
3. Spiders and birds build _____.
4. A roadrunner's head _____ straight in front when it runs.
5. The Simplon _____ goes under the Alps between Italy and Switzerland.
6. Being afraid to fly is an illogical _____.
7. We heard a loud _____ and knew that there had been an accident.
8. You can _____ my books, but please don't forget to return them.
9. Would you be _____ to meet Frankenstein?
10. Most people fly only _____.

d True/False/Not Enough Information

_____ 1. Some Eskimos are left-handed.
_____ 2. Most right-handers do calculus with the left hemisphere of the brain.
_____ 3. When people look at a beautiful building, most of them use the right hemisphere of the brain.
_____ 4. The right hemisphere controls the right side of the body.
_____ 5. Most people in the world use the left hemisphere for language.
_____ 6. Left-handedness can cause children to see letters backwards.
_____ 7. It is easier to write from left to right.
_____ 8. Left-handed people are more intelligent than right-handers.

Comprehension Questions

1. What does the right hemisphere of the brain control?
2. Which hemisphere is stronger in left-handed people?
3. Why do lefties prefer to kick with the left foot?
4. What problems do lefties have in using machines?
5. When do some left-handers start to stutter?
6. Why do anthropologists think that the earliest people were equally divided between left- and right-handers?
7. Why did the Greeks start writing from left to right?
8. What does "You are in good company" mean?
9. How can you tell if a 2-year-old child is left-handed?
10. Are you left-handed?

 Main Idea

1. What sentence is the main idea for paragraph 4 (lines 21–25)?
2. What sentence is the main idea for paragraph 6 (lines 29–34)?
3. Write a sentence for the main idea in paragraph 9 (lines 49–57).
4. Write the main idea of the last paragraph.

 Word Forms

	Verb	Noun	Adjective	Adverb
1.	communicate	communication(s)	(un)communicative	
2.	exist	existence	(non)existent	
3.	prefer	preference	(un)preferential	(un)preferentially
4.	divide	division	(in)divisible	
5.	force	force	forceful	forcefully
6.			(un)common	(un)commonly
7.	respond	response	(un)responsive	
8.	permit	permission permit	(im)permissible	(im)permissibly
9.		reality	(un)real	really

Choose a word form from the chart for each sentence below. Use the right verb forms and singular or plural nouns.

1. I tried to get the information from the president's secretary, but he was very _____.

2. Frank told everyone that he worked for a large company, but the company is _____.

3. Professors should not give _____ treatment to the students they like.

4. Ten is not evenly _____ by 3.

5. John was _____ to leave the university because his grades were so bad.

6. It is _____ believed that girls learn languages faster than boys.

7. The injured person _____ to the doctor's treatment. She is well now.

8. You cannot build a house in this city without a building _____.

9. It seemed _____ to Abdullah that he had finally finished his doctorate degree and was going home.

h Missing Words

Fill in the missing words.

1. _____ understand left-handedness, it is necessary _____ look _____ the brain.

2. The brain _____ divided _____ two hemispheres.

3. Both sides of _____ body receive the same information _____ the brain because both hemispheres _____ connected.

4. There has been _____ increasing amount _____ research _____ handedness.

5. But _____ 3500 B.C., the tools, which _____ better designed, were for use _____ only one hand.

6. _____ the centuries passed and education spread _____ more levels _____ society, more and _____ people became _____.

i Connecting Words

*Put **after, before, when, since,** or **until** in the blanks.*

1. I'll give you the book _____ I see you tomorrow.

2. People who are afraid of flying can control their fear _____ they take a class.

3. The Garbage Project has been in existence _____ 1973.

4. Toronto knew that it had done a good job recycling _____ the Garbage Project proved that the amount of its garbage had become smaller.

5. Sometimes _____ the roadrunner gets a piece of meat, it takes it back to its nest.

6. There were no skyscrapers _____ 1884.

7. _____ Burke started across Australia, he organized the expedition.

8. _____ the 1930s, teachers forced all children to write with their right hand.

Finding the Reason

Write the reason for each statement.

Statement	Reason
1. Many left-handers have to use their right hand.	
2. For some people, the center of language is in the right hemisphere.	
3. Both sides of the body receive the same information.	
4. Lefties prefer kicking with the left foot.	
5. King George VI stuttered.	
6. Anthropologists think that more than 50% of people were right-handed by 3500 B.C.	
7. Paul McCartney plays the guitar differently.	

 Guided Writing

Write one of these two short compositions.

1. Write a short history of left-handedness. Start with the earliest people and continue until today.
2. Your 3-year-old child is left-handed. Your friend thinks that you should teach the child to use the right hand instead. What are you going to do and why?

Video Highlights

a Before You Watch

1. How much do you remember about skyscrapers? Work with a partner to recall the following information from Lesson 4.

   a. The building material that made tall buildings possible:

   _____

   b. Two problems that architects and engineers had to solve:

   _____

2. Read these comments from the video "Green Skyscraper":

   "Lights, tourists, traffic. Times Square is not where you would expect to find an environmental experiment in progress."

   "But, slowly rising is a forty-eight-story building designed to save energy and other natural resources."

   Then discuss the questions below with your partner.

   a. What do you know about New York? List three facts.
   b. Why do you think this new building is called a "green skyscraper"?

b As You Watch

Listen for information that will help you complete this list:

Ways the Green Skyscraper Will Save Energy

1. It will use solar panels to generate clean _____.
2. Extra insulation will be used to keep heat (or cool air)

   _____.

3. Oversized _____ will let in light, but not too much heat.

C After You Watch

1. Check the facts. Is the underlined information in the following sentences correct? If not, change the sentence to make it correct. Write your correction above the mistake. If the information is already correct, do not change the sentence.

   Example: It's going to cut energy use by ~~80%~~ *40%* over a
              conventional building.

   a. The builder, architects, and suppliers communicate via <u>airmail</u> and the Internet.

   b. We believe we've eliminated about <u>40,000</u> sheets of paper.

   c. The building was designed to cut down on the use of <u>glass</u> and other energy-intensive building materials.

   d. Keeping buildings running takes up about <u>one half</u> of the energy used in America each year.

2. Why is the statement below important? Discuss it with a partner. Share your explanation with the class.

   "The building is going to cut energy use by 40% over a conventional building . . . . That's significant, particularly in a building this big. That's a lot of carbon dioxide (CO_2) that won't be going into the atmosphere."

Familiar Phrases

A phrase *is a group of words that has a special meaning. Use this key to figure out the familiar phrases.*

A	B	C	D	E	F	G	H	I	J	K	L	M	N	O	P	Q	R	S	T	U	V	W	X	Y	Z
Z	Y	X	W	V	U	T	S	R	Q	P	O	N	M	L	K	J	I	H	G	F	E	D	C	B	A

Write the phrase on the top line, and then use it in a sentence of your own on the bottom line.

Example: R M   T L L W   X K N Z M B

in good company

If you like to swim, you are in good company with fish.

1. G Z K   B L F I   U L L G

_____

_____

2. Z   S R T S - I R H V   Y F R O W R M T

_____

_____

3. L M X V   R M   Z   D S R O V

_____

_____

Dictionary Page

Understanding Grammar Codes

1. You can use your dictionary to learn about regular verbs.

Ending	Form	Example
-ed	simple past	They designed the building to save energy.
-ed	past participle	The building was designed to save energy.
-ing	present participle	The architects are designing a new building.
-s	third person singular	He designs buildings for a living.

Your dictionary also gives you the forms of all irregular verbs. Look at this entry for the verb *swim*. Label each of its main forms.

past simple

swim /swɪm/ *v.* **swam** /swæm/, **swum** /swʌm/, **swimming, swims 1** [I] to move through water by moving parts of the body (legs, arms, fins, tails): *He swam across the river and back again.*

2. Complete these sentences with the correct form of the verb in parentheses. Use your dictionary to check for the correct spelling.

Example: The audience (clap) <u>clapped</u> their hands and stamped their feet.

a. The Taipei 101 building (steal) _____ the title of "tallest building in the world."

b. I (lose) _____ my wallet somewhere.

c. Many left-handers (excel) _____ in tennis, baseball, and swimming.

Science

Minds are like parachutes. They only function when they are open.
—**Sir James Dewar**

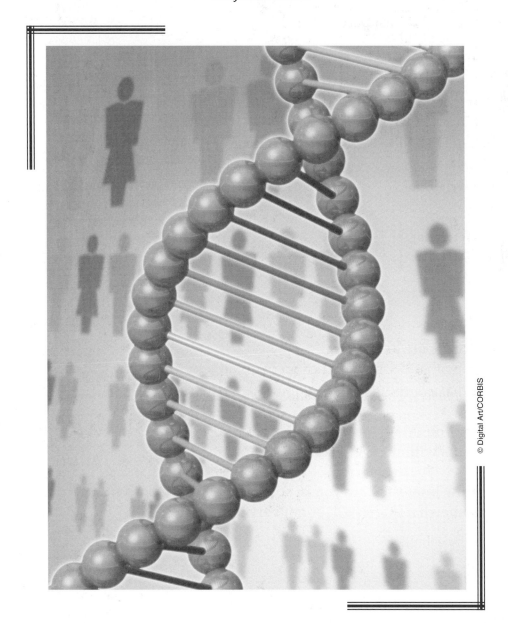

© Digital Art/CORBIS

lesson

1

Biospheres in Space

© James Marshall/CORBIS

Before You Read

1. What might this building be used for?

2. Do you think you could live inside this building for two years without ever leaving it?

3. How interested are you in space travel—very interested, somewhat interested, or not very interested?

Context Clues

*The words in **bold** print are from this lesson. Use context clues to guess the meaning of each word.*

1. Will it ever be possible for people to live on faraway **planets** such as Mars and Jupiter?

2. Scientists at the Environmental Research **Laboratory** are doing experiments on the Earth's environment.

3. A biosphere will need **bacteria** or something else to take care of the wastes.

4. **So far,** only a few experimental biospheres have been built on Earth.

1 Biospheres in Space

Will it ever be possible for people to live on faraway **planets** such as Mars? In the past, **colonies** in space were possible only in **science fiction** stories. Today, however, we are experimenting with ways to build real space
5   colonies. Many scientists actually **consider** it possible that people will live far from the Earth sometime in the future.

planets

The Environmental Research **Laboratory** at the University of Arizona is one place that designs biospheres (*bio* means *life,* and a *sphere* is a *circle,* like a
10   ball) which could be used to live on other planets. Biospheres are complete, enclosed environments where people can be born, live their whole lives, and die without returning to the Earth. To be successful, a biosphere has to have a perfect **balance** among
15   everything within it—the plants, the animals (including humans), and the chemical **elements.** Specialists and experts from many different fields are needed to work on these **complex** projects.

complicated

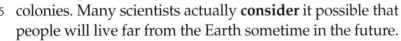

169

Building a greenhouse for growing plants in winter
20 is the first step in **creating** a biosphere. A greenhouse   making
is a closed environment except for the sun's heat
entering through the glass or plastic. Of course, there is
a water system from outside, and people bring in
nutrients for the plants and take out the waste material.
25 A biosphere in space will have to have its own system
to provide water that can be used and reused. It will
need **bacteria** or something else to take care of the
wastes. Everything must be perfectly balanced, or else
the whole system will break down.
30   The Earth itself is the best example of a real
biosphere. Nothing important enters except sunlight,
and nothing leaves as waste except some heat.
Everything in the Earth's environment needs to be in
balance. If we destroy that balance, the system will
35 break down.

There are several reasons for building biospheres.
One reason is to help out when there is an energy
shortage. Dr. Gerard K. O'Neill, a famous **physicist**
from Princeton University, has said that in the future we

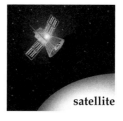

satellite

40 will have **satellites** in space to produce **solar** energy   of the sun
and send it to the Earth. It will be too expensive to
continually send people and materials to the satellites,
so biospheres will be necessary. He thinks that 10,000
people could live in a space colony sometime in the
45 future. There is another interesting reason to build
biospheres. We can use them to do all kinds of research
about our own environment and how it works. By
studying biospheres, we can understand better what
will happen as humans destroy tropical forests, as they
50 create more **carbon dioxide** by burning fuel, and as they
pollute the oceans and the air.

<u>So far,</u> only a few experimental biospheres have   until now
been built on Earth. One is in Oracle, Arizona, near the
University of Arizona. In 1991, four men and four
55 women tried to live inside the biosphere without
getting anything from outside. During the experiment,
things got out of balance. Oxygen and carbon dioxide
levels fell, and the crew had to get help and supplies

170

from outside. In space, people living in a biosphere
60 would not be able to do this.

　　　Learning how a biosphere works is one of the most
important things we can do. The information we get
from biospheres may **keep** us **from** destroying our own
environment. This information will also help us to
65 travel where once only science fiction could go.

a　Vocabulary

colony	planet	project	science fiction
solar	satellite	complex	balance
physicist	bacteria	consider	carbon dioxide

1. The Earth is a _____. It is part of the
   _____ system.
2. _____ can cause disease. They also destroy wastes.
3. Ants live together in a _____.
4. Julia likes to read _____.
5. It's difficult to _____ a book on your head while you
   are walking.
6. The government's biggest _____ is to build a dam to store
   water for agriculture.
7. Another word for *complicated* is _____.
8. We must _____ the advantages and the disadvantages
   before we start the project.

b Vocabulary

create	satellite	bacteria	carbon dioxide
so far	keep	laboratory	elements
balance	project	physicist	consider

1. CO_2 stands for _____.
2. Gold (Au), oxygen (O), and uranium (U) are all _____.
3. Destroying rain forests can _____ problems for the whole world.
4. Scientists in a _____ often wear white coats.
5. _____, there are no buildings over 120 stories high.
6. A _____ teaches or does research in physics.
7. Before the large increase in population, there was a _____ between the needs of the people and what the land could produce.
8. Much international communication is now done by _____.
9. Designing a space colony would be a difficult _____.
10. They locked the door to _____ people from coming in.
11. I _____ you to be a good friend.

c Vocabulary Review

diet	tools	clockwise	story
takes off	dispose of	harmful	phobia
straighten	position	permission	remained

1. You need to turn the door knob _____ in order to open the door.
2. You should turn off your cell phone before the plane _____.
3. It's not healthy to live on a _____ of junk food.
4. If they _____ the road, people will drive a lot faster.
5. Smoking is _____ to your health.
6. His office is on the twenty-sixth floor of a forty-_____ building.
7. What _____ do you need to build a house?

8. You need to get special _____ to go inside the laboratory.

9. How would people in a space colony _____ their garbage?

10. Only three people _____ in the theater to see the whole movie. Everyone else left early.

d Multiple Choice

1. Fiction is _____.
   a. true
   b. imaginative
   c. boring

2. Biospheres are complicated projects because _____.
   a. everything must be perfectly balanced
   b. scientists don't know what materials to use to build them
   c. people from different professions work on them

3. The experimental biosphere in Arizona _____.
   a. was very successful
   b. had serious problems
   c. stayed in perfect balance

4. Biospheres in space could support _____ people.
   a. two or three
   b. ten
   c. 10,000

5. A greenhouse _____.
   a. is a partly enclosed environment
   b. is a biosphere
   c. supports plant life independently

6. _____ might take care of the wastes in a biosphere.
   a. A water system
   b. Balanced nutrients
   c. Bacteria

7. Dr. O'Neill thinks that _____.
   a. satellites can produce solar energy
   b. about ten people could take care of a satellite
   c. we need a space colony to study the solar system

Comprehension Questions

1. Why is it a complex project to create a biosphere?
2. How is a greenhouse different from a biosphere?
3. Explain why the Earth is a biosphere.
4. How does Dr. O'Neill think that we will solve the energy shortage?
5. Why can we learn about our environment from a biosphere?
6. What happened when people moved into the Arizona biosphere?
7. Would you like to live in a biosphere on Mars? Why or why not?

 Main Idea

1. What is the main idea of paragraph 4 (lines 30–35)?
2. What is the main idea of paragraph 5 (lines 36–51)?
3. Write a sentence that gives the main idea for paragraph 6 (lines 52–60).

g Cause and Effect

What is the cause of each of these effects?

Cause	Effect
1.	People can live their whole lives in biospheres.
2.	The whole system might break down.
3.	The same water must be used and reused.
4.	We will need solar energy.
5.	A biosphere will be necessary to run solar energy production.
6.	We create more carbon dioxide.

Word Forms: Verbs and Nouns

Many English words are used as both a verb and a noun. Use ten of these examples in sentences, using some verbs and some nouns.

Verb	Noun
balance	balance
crash	crash
force	force
design	design
escape	escape
party	party
fear	fear
harm	harm
bother	bother
whistle	whistle
knock	knock

 ## Noun Substitutes

What do these noun substitutes stand for?

1. page 170 line 26 **it** _____
2. page 170 line 41 **it** _____
3. page 170 line 46 **them** _____
4. page 170 line 47 **it** _____
5. page 170 line 53 **one** _____

Articles

Put articles in the blanks if they are necessary.

1. _____ Environmental Research Laboratory at _____ University of Arizona is one place that designs _____ biospheres.

2. _____ greenhouse is _____ closed environment except for _____ sun's heat entering through the glass.

3. _____ Earth itself is _____ best example of _____ real biosphere.

4. Everything in _____ Earth's environment needs to be in _____ balance.

5. So far, only _____ few experimental biospheres have been built on _____ Earth.

6. Oxygen levels fell, and _____ crew had to get _____ help and _____ supplies from outside.

7. Learning how _____ biosphere works is one of _____ most important things we can do.

 Guided Writing

Write one of these two short compositions.

1. Should we build biospheres? Why or why not?
2. You are living in a biosphere on Mars. Describe your life.

lesson 2

Earthquakes

© Roger Ressmeyer/CORBIS

Before You Read

1. What happened in this picture?

2. Have you ever felt an earthquake?

3. What should you do if you feel an earthquake?

177

Context Clues

*The words in **bold** print are from this lesson. Use context clues to guess the meaning of each word.*

1. A large movement causes a violent earthquake, but a small movement causes a **mild** one.

2. When the ocean waves hit land, they **flood** coastal areas.

3. During the earthquake, bridges fell and cars were **crushed.**

4. Estimates of deaths **ranged** from 250,000 to 695,000.

5. **Seismology** is the study of earthquakes.

2   Earthquakes

What causes earthquakes? The outer <u>layer</u> of the Earth is divided into huge pieces that are constantly moving. When two of the pieces move against each other or move in opposite directions, an earthquake
5 happens. A large movement causes a violent earthquake, and a small movement causes a **mild** one. There are thousands of earthquakes every year, but most of them are very small.

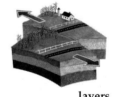

layers

The place where an earthquake begins is called the
10 **epicenter.** When an earthquake happens, <u>vibrations</u> move outward from the epicenter. These **rolling** vibrations are called **seismic** waves. Usually, an earthquake is only strong enough to cause damage near its epicenter.

shaking movements

When the epicenter of an earthquake is at the bottom
15 of the ocean, it can create huge sea waves as tall as fifteen meters. These waves cross the ocean in several hours. Rushing toward land, they destroy small islands and ships in their path. When they hit land, they <u>flood</u> coastal areas far from the epicenter of the earthquake. In
20 1868, a wave reached 4.5 kilometers inland in Peru.

cover with water

After an earthquake happens, people can die from lack of food, water, and medical supplies. The amount of destruction caused by an earthquake depends on where it happens, what time it happens, and how strong it is. It also depends on the types of buildings in the area, the soil conditions, and the size of the population. Of the thousands of earthquakes in the world each year, only about 1 in 500 causes damage.

In 1556, an earthquake in northern China killed 830,000 people—the most in history. At that time, there was no way to measure its strength. In 1935, scientists started using the Richter Scale to measure seismic waves. A seriously destructive earthquake measures 6.5 or higher on the Richter Scale.

How can scientists predict earthquakes? Earthquakes are not just **scattered** anywhere on the surface of the Earth; they happen in areas where pieces of the Earth's surface meet. For example, earthquakes often occur on the west coasts of North and South America, around the Mediterranean Sea, and along the Pacific coast of Asia.

One way to predict earthquakes is to look for changes in the Earth's surface, like a sudden drop in the water level in the ground. Some people say that animals can predict earthquakes. Before earthquakes, people have seen chickens sitting in trees, fish jumping out of the water, snakes leaving their holes, and other animals acting strangely.

On February 4, 1975, scientists predicted an earthquake in northeastern China and told people in the earthquake zone to leave the cities. More than a million people moved into the surrounding countryside, into safe, open fields away from buildings. That afternoon, the ground rolled and shook beneath the people's feet. In seconds, 90% of the buildings in the city of Haicheng were destroyed. The decision to tell the people to leave the cities saved 10,000 lives.

However, more than a year later, on July 28, 1976, the scientists were not so lucky. East of Beijing, Chinese scientists were discussing a possible earthquake. During their meeting, the worst earthquake in modern times hit. Estimates of deaths **ranged** from 250,000 to 695,000.

179

The earthquake measured 7.9 on the Richter Scale.

In late 1984, strong earthquakes began shaking the Nevado del Ruiz **volcano** in Colombia. On November 14, 1985, the volcano finally **erupted.** A nearby river became a sea of mud that buried four towns, and more than 2,100 people were killed. This combination of an earthquake and a volcanic eruption was not a **unique**   one of a kind
event. In fact, it's not unusual for earthquakes and volcanic eruptions to happen at the same time.

Mexico City has frequent earthquakes. An earthquake there on September 19, 1985, measured 8.1 on the Richter Scale and killed 7,000 people. Most **victims** died when buildings fell on them.

volcano

San Francisco, California, also has frequent earthquakes. However, newer buildings there are built to be safe in earthquakes. When an earthquake measuring 7.1 on the Richter Scale hit northern California on October 17, 1989, only 67 people were killed. The earthquake hit in the afternoon, when thousands of people were driving home from work. Freeways and bridges broke and fell. Buried under the layers of the Oakland Freeway, people were **crushed** in their flattened cars. Explosions sounded like **thunder** as older buildings seemed to **burst** apart along with the freeways. As electric power lines were broken by the falling bridges and buildings, the sky, covered with huge clouds of black dust, appeared to be filled with

lightning

lightning. Water from broken pipes rushed into the streets and mixed with gas from broken gas lines, causing more explosions.

Emergency workers had to **cope** with medical problems. Everyone worked together to save survivors and comfort victims. The next day, the disaster sites looked terrible. Victims couldn't find their houses, their cars, or even their streets. Boats were destroyed, and **debris** covered the surface of the sea. There was no   trash
water, no electricity, no telephone service, only the smell of garbage **floating** in **melted** ice in refrigerators open to the sun. Losses and **property** damage from the earthquake amounted to millions of dollars.

Seismology is the study of earthquakes, and a seismologist is a scientist who **observes** earthquakes.
105 Seismologists have given us valuable knowledge about earthquakes. Their equipment measures the smallest vibrations on the surface of the Earth. They are trying to find ways to use knowledge about earthquakes to save lives and to help solve the world's energy
110 shortage. The Earth's natural activity underground creates energy in the form of heat. **Geothermal** means *earth heat*.

If seismologists could predict earthquakes, we could save about 20,000 human lives each year.
115 Humans can control many things about nature, but they cannot control earthquakes.

a Vocabulary

volcanoes	rolled	floods	unique
vibrate	thunder	erupted	crush
victim	lightning	bursts	melts
float	layer	geothermal	mild

1. When snow _____ in the mountains, it can cause _____ in the lowlands.

2. Earthquakes can happen before the eruption of _____.

3. _____ energy comes from heat under the Earth.

4. Mount St. Helens, a volcano in Washington State in the United States, _____ in 1980.

5. When Peter set his pencil down, it _____ off onto the floor.

6. A blowout happens when a tire _____ while a car is moving.

7. The weather has been _____ this week. Even though it is winter, it hasn't been very cold.

8. They built their house themselves, so it's truly _____.

9. There are both heat and activity below the outer _____ of the Earth.

10. A storm with both _____ and _____ is sometimes called an electrical storm.

b Vocabulary

layer	scattered	floating	roll
observe	debris	ranges	seismology
victim	cope	crushed	thunder
vibration	epicenter	property	unique

1. After the huge wave sank the ship, all you could see was some

   _____ _____ on the surface of the sea.

2. The wind _____ my papers all over the room.

3. In a rain forest, the lower _____ of plant growth is

   protected by the upper one.

4. Students who plan to become teachers usually have to

   _____ classes as a first step toward teaching.

5. The freeway bridge fell down because it was near the

   _____ of the earthquake. Its weight _____

   many cars.

6. When we stand near a busy freeway, we can feel the _____

   of the traffic under our feet.

7. The yearly pay of an engineer _____ from $17,000

   to $75,000.

8. Mr. Dahood used to be a rich man, but he was a _____ of

   the earthquake and lost all of his _____.

9. Sometimes when people have serious problems, they cannot

   _____ with them.

10. _____ has helped us find possible earthquake sites.

c Vocabulary Review

Write the correct synonym and antonym for each word in the chart.

Synonyms

answer	small	dangerous	pick up
complicated	make	take away	balance
consider	allow	until now	wide

Antonyms

uncomplicated	give	forbid	safe
ignore	drop	not yet	actual
narrow	unit	destroy	huge

	Synonyms	Antonyms
1. lift	*pick up*	*drop*
2. complex		
3. so far		
4. create		
5. respond		
6. steal		
7. broad		
8. hazardous		
9. tiny		
10. permit		

d True/False/Not Enough Information

_____ 1. Today, scientists know something about the causes of earthquakes.

_____ 2. Most earthquakes cause a lot of property damage.

_____ 3. More than half of the world's earthquakes are too small to cause serious damage.

_____ 4. More people are killed by huge sea waves than by falling buildings.

_____ 5. Seismologists can measure the size of seismic waves.

_____ 6. Removing water from the ground causes earthquakes.

_____ 7. Most of the world's earthquakes are mild.

_____ 8. An earthquake in 1989 destroyed the city of Oakland.

_____ 9. People can predict earthquakes by studying the weather.

_____ 10. *Thermal* means *heat*.

e Comprehension Questions

1. How does movement in the Earth cause earthquakes?
2. What is the epicenter of an earthquake? What is a seismic wave?
3. Why does most of the damage from an earthquake happen near the epicenter?
4. Why are earthquakes dangerous when they happen in the middle of the ocean?
5. What can you look for to predict an earthquake?
6. What was lucky about the earthquake that happened in northeastern China in 1975?
7. How can people protect themselves and their property from earthquakes?
8. Why do people continue to live where there are earthquakes?

f Paraphrasing

Use your own words to combine the ideas in these two sentences from the text. It is not necessary to use the same number of sentences. You may use more.

Usually, an earthquake is strong enough to cause damage only near its epicenter.

The amount of destruction caused by an earthquake depends on where it happens, what time it happens, and how strong it is.

g Main Idea

Write or copy a sentence that is the main idea for these paragraphs.

1. Paragraph 3 (lines 14–20)
2. Paragraph 8 (lines 49–57)
3. Paragraph 10 (lines 64–71)

184

 Word Forms

Choose a word form from the chart for each sentence below. Use the right verb forms and singular or plural nouns.

	Verb	Noun	Adjective	Adverb
1.	respond	response	responsive	responsively
2.	consider	consideration	(in)considerate	(in)considerately
3.		complexity	complex	
4.	educate	education	educational	
5.	create	creation creativity	(un)creative	creatively
6.	value	value	valuable	
7.	observe	observation observatory	(un)observant	
8.	specialize	specialist	special	
9.	explain	explanation	(un)explainable	
10.	believe	belief	(un)believable	(un)believably

1. The police _____ immediately to our call for help.
2. Marge is a very _____ person. She thinks of others and what they want, instead of thinking of herself most of the time.
3. The _____ of modern society affects family life.
4. There are a few _____ programs on TV.
5. Pablo Picasso was a very _____ artist. He was known for his _____.
6. Most people want to have friends. They _____ the friendship of people they like.
7. After the director of the English program _____ classes, she writes up her _____.
8. She wants to be a doctor who _____ in childhood diseases.

 185

9. Can scientists give a clear _____ of what actually happens deep in the Earth? No, some of the details are _____ so far.

10. Scientists consider it _____ that gods create volcanic eruptions.

i   Scanning

Scan the text to find this information. Write a short answer and the number of the line where you found the information.

1. In 1975, what percentage of the buildings in the city of Haicheng were destroyed? _____

2. What did the Mexico City earthquake measure on the Richter Scale?
   _____

3. What time of day did the earthquake hit northern California in October 1989? _____

4. What is the largest number of people killed in an earthquake?
   _____

j   Two-Word Verbs

Learn these two-word verbs and then fill in the blanks with the right words. Use the correct verb form. Numbers 2 and 3 use the same expression twice.

mix up	= mistake one thing for another
dress up	= put on special clothes
have on	= be wearing
look out	= be careful
spread out	= spread over a certain area or time

1. Don't try to learn forty irregular verbs in one day. _____ them _____ over a week or two.

2. People usually _____ for a party. Children like to _____ in their parents' old clothes and pretend that they are adults.

3. She _____ her homework assignments and gave the reading homework to the wrong teacher. Then she found out that she had done the wrong page. She was _____.

4. _____! There's a child in the street!

5. Mike _____ his running clothes because he was going to exercise.

k Sequencing

Put these sentences about the October 17, 1989, earthquake in the right order. Number 1 is done for you.

_____ a. Freeways and bridges broke and fell.

_____ b. As electric power lines broke, the dark sky seemed to be full of lightning.

__1__ c. People were driving home in their cars in the afternoon after work.

_____ d. Buildings exploded and pipes broke.

_____ e. Water and gas from broken lines mixed and exploded.

_____ f. The Earth began to shake and roll.

_____ g. People died in their cars when freeways and bridges fell on top of them.

_____ h. Huge clouds of black dust began to cover the sky.

_____ i. Victims could find nothing when they came back.

_____ j. Emergency workers hurried to find survivors and save victims.

l Summarizing

Summarize paragraph 9, lines 58–63. Use your own words to tell the main idea.

m Guided Writing

Write one of these two short compositions.

1. You are in a city when an earthquake hits. Describe what happens. Tell what you feel, see, hear, and smell.
2. You are a seismologist. Tell what scientific information you know about earthquakes. Include how and where they happen and what you are studying right now.

Snow and Hail

lesson

3

© Bettmann/CORBIS

Before You Read

1. What is the difference between snow and hail?

2. What problems can snow and hail cause?

3. Do you like to look at snow? Do you like to be outside in it?

Context Clues

*The words in **bold** print are from this lesson. Use context clues to guess the meaning of each word.*

1. This happens in the **atmosphere**, ten kilometers above the Earth.

2. This sounds **simple**, but it is actually very complex.

3. Hail is a small round ball of **alternating** layers of snow and clear ice.

4. All snowflakes are six-sided, but no one understands why this is **so**.

3 Snow and Hail

Millions of people in the world have never seen snow. Others see more of it than they want to. Hail is much more common; it <u>occurs</u> even in deserts.

happens

Each tiny piece of snow is called a **snowflake,** and
5   each flake has six sides or six points. Billions of snowflakes fall every winter, and the <u>astonishing</u> fact is that each one is different. A snowflake is as individual as someone's handwriting or <u>fingerprint</u>.

amazing

A snowflake forms inside a winter storm cloud
10   when a **microscopic** piece of dust is <u>trapped</u> inside a tiny drop of water. This happens in the <u>atmosphere</u>, ten kilometers above the Earth. The water freezes around the dust, and as this flake is blown by the wind, it collects more drops of water. These drops freeze too,
15   and the snowflake becomes heavy enough to fall to the Earth. As it falls, it passes through areas where the temperature and humidity vary. It collects more and more tiny drops of water, and the shape continually changes. Some drops fall off and start to form
20   new snowflakes.

not able to escape
air around the Earth

fingerprint

This sounds **simple,** but it is actually very complex. It is so complex that **mathematicians** using computers are just beginning to understand what happens. Every change in temperature and humidity in the air
25 around the snowflake causes a change in the speed and **pattern** of the snowflake's formation as it makes its trip to the Earth. Since no two flakes follow exactly the same path to the ground, no two snowflakes are exactly alike. However, they are all six-sided. So far, no one
30 understands why this is <u>**so.**</u>   true

Hail is a small round ball of **alternating** layers of snow and clear ice. It forms inside thunderclouds. There are two theories about how hailstones form.

One theory says that hail forms when drops of water
35 freeze in the upper air. As they fall, they collect more drops of water, just as snowflakes do. They also collect snow. The ice and snow build up in layers. If you cut a hailstone, you can see these alternating layers.

The other theory says that hail starts as a raindrop.
40 The wind carries it higher into the atmosphere, where it gets covered by snow. It becomes heavy and begins to fall. As it falls, it gets a new layer of water, which freezes. Then the wind carries it back up to the snow region, and it gets another layer of snow. This can
45 happen **multiple** times. Finally, the hailstone is too   many; a number of
heavy to travel on the wind, and it falls to the ground.

Only thunderstorms can produce hail, but very few of them do. Perhaps only one in 400 thunderstorms creates hailstones. Hail <u>**ordinarily**</u> falls in a strip from   usually
50 ten to twenty kilometers wide and <u>**up to**</u> forty   no more than
kilometers long.

A hailstone is usually less than eight centimeters in diameter. However, hailstones can be much bigger than that. Sometimes they are as big as baseballs. The largest
55 hailstone ever recorded weighed over 680 grams and had a diameter of thirteen centimeters.

Hail can do a lot of damage to agriculture, especially since hail usually appears in <u>**mid**</u>summer, when the   the middle of
plants are partly grown. If the crops are destroyed, it is
60 too late to plant more, and the farmer has lost

everything. The most damage is done by hailstones that are only the size of peas. In one terrible hailstorm in 1923 in Rostov, in Ukraine, twenty-three people and many cattle were killed.

65   Snow can cause damage too. It can cave in the roof of a building. A heavy snowstorm can delay airplane flights and cause automobile accidents. Farm animals sometimes die in snowstorms, and when country roads are closed by snow, people can be trapped in their cars
70 and freeze to death. Yet there is nothing more beautiful than the sight of millions of snowflakes falling at night. That is when people think of the beauty, and not the science, of snowflakes.

a Vocabulary

ordinarily	mathematics	midsummer	traps
so	atmosphere	snowflake	microscopic
alternating	multiple	up to	fingerprint

1. Hail falls in a strip _____ forty kilometers long.

2. In _____, the study of lines, angles, and shapes is called geometry.

3. The weather is usually warm or hot in _____.

4. Some people use _____ to catch animals.

5. Some people still believe that volcanic eruptions are caused by angry gods, but we know this isn't _____.

6. Every _____ has six sides.

7. The boys and girls lined up in _____ rows.

8. Bacteria are _____. They can't be seen without a microscope.

9. There are _____ reasons to study earthquakes, not just one.

b Vocabulary

occur	fingerprint	up to	atmosphere
ordinarily	hail	so	pattern
trap	microscope	simply	astonished

1. I was _____ that I was able to lift 100 pounds. I never thought I could.

2. When did the last eruption of Kilauea _____?

3. The police _____ criminals.

4. There is a _____ to her behavior. She's always happy in the morning and sad in the evening.

5. Humans are polluting the Earth's _____.

6. That's a difficult question. I really can't answer it _____.

7. _____ he leaves for work late, but today he's leaving early.

8. _____ can destroy a farmer's crops.

c Vocabulary Review: Definitions

Match each word with its definition.

_____	1. observe	a. movement of the Earth
_____	2. so far	b. also
_____	3. in addition	c. ÷
_____	4. earthquake	d. top layer
_____	5. story	e. CO_2
_____	6. prefer	f. floor
_____	7. divide	g. fiction
_____	8. respond	h. of the sun
_____	9. permit	i. watch
_____	10. surface	j. answer
_____	11. carbon dioxide	k. like better
_____	12. solar	l. allow
		m. until now

d Short Answers

*Write **hail, snow,** or **hail and snow** after each of these sentences.*

1. As it is blown by the wind, it collects water. _____
2. It occurs only in the colder regions of the world. _____
3. It is formed of layers of ice and snow. _____
4. It can destroy crops. _____
5. It can cause the death of humans. _____
6. It is sometimes formed around a piece of dust. _____
7. It always has six sides or points. _____
8. It is produced only by thunderstorms. _____
9. It is a small round ball. _____
10. It can cause damage. _____

e Comprehension Questions

1. Why do all snowflakes have six sides or six points?
2. Snowflakes start forming around two things. What are they?
3. What does a change in humidity do to the formation of a snowflake?
4. Why are no two snowflakes alike?
5. Where do hailstones form?
6. What causes both snowflakes and hail to fall to the ground?
7. How big is the average hailstone?
8. How does hail destroy crops?
9. Give an example of how snow can be destructive.
10. Which is more destructive, hail or snow? Why?
11. Do roadrunners ever see hail?

f Main Idea

1. Write a sentence for the main idea of paragraph 2 (lines 4–8).
2. Write a sentence for the main idea of paragraph 4 (lines 21–30).
3. Which sentence is the main idea of paragraph 10 (lines 57–64)?

g Word Forms: Negative Prefixes

These are common negative prefixes. Put a word from Number 1 in the first sentence below, and so on. Use the right form of the word.

1. **dis-:** dislike, discomfort, displease, disconnect, dishonest
2. **un-:** unequipped, uncreative, unprepared, unobservant
3. **non-:** nonsmoking, nonalcoholic, nonviolent, nonindustrial
4. **in-:** inactive, inconsiderate, incorrect, inexpensive
5. **im-:** impossible, improbable, immovable, imperfect
6. **il-:** illogical, illiterate
7. **ir-:** irregular, irreligious
8. **mis-:** misbehave, misspell, misunderstand, misspeak

1. Alice always _____ the television during a thunderstorm.
2. Bering and his men were _____ for living on the island after their boat sank.
3. Coke and Pepsi are _____ drinks.
4. It is _____ to eat something in front of someone else and not offer him or her some.
5. It is _____ to squeeze water out of a stone.
6. It is _____ to think that someone who is _____ is unintelligent.
7. _____ verbs must be memorized.
8. There are three _____ words in your homework paper.

h Articles

Put articles in the blanks if they are needed.

1. _____ snowflake forms inside _____ winter storm cloud when _____ microscopic piece of dust is trapped inside _____ tiny drop of _____ water.
2. This happens in _____ atmosphere, ten kilometers above _____ Earth.

3. _____ water freezes around _____ dust, and as this flake is blown by _____ wind, it collects more drops of _____ water.

4. As it falls, it passes through _____ areas where _____ temperature and _____ humidity vary.

5. It is so complex that _____ mathematicians using _____ computers are just beginning to understand what happens.

6. Every change in _____ temperature and _____ humidity in _____ air causes _____ change in _____ speed and _____ pattern of _____ snowflake's formation as it makes its trip to _____ Earth.

7. _____ hail is _____ small round ball of _____ alternating layers of _____ snow and _____ clear ice.

i ☐ Compound Words

Make a one-word or two-word compound using a word from the first column and one from the second.

_____	1. sky	a. sign
_____	2. science	b. surgery
_____	3. thunder	c. storm
_____	4. traffic	d. walk
_____	5. diet	e. scraper
_____	6. ground	f. force
_____	7. brain	g. floor
_____	8. work	h. branch
_____	9. side	i. fiction
_____	10. tree	j. plan

j ☐ Summarizing

Write a summary of the information about snow. Write five or six sentences.

k Guided Writing

Write one of these two short compositions.

1. Compare snow and hail.
2. Describe a serious winter storm that you experienced or heard about.

lesson 4
Photovoltaic Cells: Energy Source of the Future

© Andy Hibbert; Ecoscene/CORBIS

Before You Read

1. What is solar energy?

2. Do you have anything with you right now that works by solar energy? If so, what is it?

3. How do we produce electricity? Name as many ways as you know.

Context Clues

*The words in **bold** print below are from the reading in this lesson. Use context clues to guess the meaning of each word.*

1. A **conductor** is something that electricity can pass through. Water and metals conduct electricity, but wood does not.

2. Another advantage is that it is **solid-state;** that is, there are no moving parts.

3. If the top gets dusty, less light enters, and it doesn't work as **efficiently** as it should.

4. Developing countries cannot export enough agricultural products and other **raw materials.**

4 Photovoltaic Cells: Energy Source of the Future

As populations increase and countries industrialize, the world's demand for energy increases. Our supply of petroleum and gas is limited, but the **photovoltaic cell** offers a solution to the problem of a future energy
5 shortage. This cell is already an important source of energy. In fact, it seems almost like **magic.** The photovoltaic cell changes sunlight directly into energy. Solar energy—energy from the sun—is clean, easily available, <u>**inexhaustible,**</u> and free, if the equipment
10 is available.

without end; limitless

Did you ever reach to open the door at a store or hotel and see it open by itself? Does your camera always let in the right amount of light for your pictures? These are examples of uses of photovoltaic cells. They
15 are also used in calculators and watches, in remote telecommunication units, and in central power stations to produce electricity. Another important use is in the space exploration program. This program could not **exist** without the energy produced by photovoltaic cells.

20   The photovoltaic cell is simple. It has **transparent**   able to be seen
    metallic film at the top. Below this is a layer of **silicon.**   through
    A metal base is at the bottom.

    The sunlight falls on the **boundary** between the two
    different types of **semiconductors** in the photovoltaic
25   cell, the silicon and the metal base. A **conductor** is
    something that electricity can pass through. Water and
    metals conduct electricity, but wood does not. A
    semiconductor conducts electricity poorly at low
    temperatures, but when heat or light is added,
30   conductivity is increased.

    As the light falls on this boundary between the two
    types of semiconductors, it creates an electric current.
    The sunlight is **converted** directly into electricity.   changed

    One advantage of the photovoltaic cell is that it is
35   **solid-state;** that is, there are no moving parts. **Since**   because
    there are no moving parts to break down, the cell will
    last a long time if it is protected from damage. This
    protection is important. If the top of the cell gets dusty,
    less light enters, and the cell doesn't work as **efficiently**
40   as it should.

    In addition, silicon is one of the most common
    elements in the world; for example, sand is made up
    mostly of silicon. At one time, the chemical preparation
    of silicon for use in a photovoltaic cell was very
45   expensive. Now the cost has gone down a great deal.
    Scientists have also found a way to produce silicon in
    long sheets, similar to the way plastic for plastic bags is
    made today. This is helping the cost of a unit of solar
    energy to fall even more. Today, there are large factories
50   using solar-cell systems in a number of countries.

    About 18% of the sunlight that reaches the
    photovoltaic cell is converted into electricity. This is a
    small amount, so many cells must be used to create a
    reasonable amount of electricity. However, technology
55   can be developed to make the cells more efficient and
    raise the percentage of sunlight converted to 27%.

    What does solar energy mean to the world?
    Photovoltaic cells have several advantages over fossil
    fuels (gas, oil, and coal). Fossil fuels that we use today

60 were formed from plants and animals that lived millions of years ago. Those plants and animals were able to exist because of the sun. Obviously, we can't wait a million years for more fossil fuels. The photovoltaic cell gives us the ability to produce energy
65 directly from the sun. The sun's energy can be converted for our use immediately.

At the present time, gas and oil are expensive. Developing countries cannot **export** enough agricultural products and other **raw materials** to allow them to
70 **import** the fuel that they need to produce energy. At the same time, petroleum supplies are limited, and in a few decades, they will run out. However, the supply of sunlight is limitless, and most of the poor countries of the world are in the tropics, where there is plenty of
75 sunlight.

sell to other countries

The photovoltaic cell has another very important advantage. It is a clean source of energy. The fossil fuels that we use today are the main source of the pollution in our atmosphere.

80 Although many individuals and governments have been **reluctant** to reduce their dependence on fossil fuels, there is a growing market for solar energy. There is even discussion of collecting solar energy on satellites and then beaming it to Earth. This process is called
85 Space Solar Power. If we truly want cheaper and better ways to create energy, solar power offers many possibilities.

hesitant; afraid; unwilling

a Vocabulary

photovoltaic cell	inexhaustible	silicon	semiconductors
solid-state	reluctant	import	exports
magic	raw material	reasonable	exist

1. Scientists think that the _____ will be an important energy source for the future.
2. The number of snowflakes is limitless and _____.
3. A photovoltaic cell has two different types of _____.
4. Many people are _____ to try new things.
5. Do you know how many kinds of birds _____ in the world today?
6. Children like to see _____ shows.
7. Japan _____ television sets but has to _____ oil.
8. _____ is used to make glass.
9. Iron is the main _____ for making steel.

b Vocabulary

exist	reluctant	since	efficient
magical	export	reasonable	transparent
boundary	import	conducts	converts

1. Electric current can pass through metal because metal _____ electricity.
2. He was _____ to drive at first, but now he loves to drive.
3. Much of the _____ between Canada and the United States is a straight line.
4. Abdullah missed the test _____ he was late for class.
5. Thirty minutes is a _____ length of time for a short test.
6. There is something _____ about watching the sun rise.
7. It is more _____ for thirty people to ride in a bus than in thirty different cars.

8. Glass is _____.

9. A hydroelectric power station _____ water power
   into electricity.

c Vocabulary Review

Underline the word that does not belong with the others.

1. hail, snowflake, trap, rain
2. create, damage, destroy, harm
3. definite, sure, exact, bacteria
4. satellite, planet, star, sun
5. consider, object, discuss, talk over
6. backwards, forward, clockwise, sideward
7. physicist, anthropologist, chemist, geologist
8. burst, eruption, flood, earthquake
9. fly, bee, ant, snake

d Multiple Choice

1. Solar energy will not be _____ in the future.
   a. expensive
   b. easily available
   c. limitless

2. Sunlight first enters a photovoltaic cell through _____.
   a. a metal base
   b. metallic film
   c. a layer of silicon

3. The place where the two semiconductors meet is called the _____.
   a. border
   b. conductor
   c. boundary

4. A semiconductor works best when _____.
   a. there is wood available
   b. the temperature is low
   c. light or heat is added

5. A photovoltaic cell _____ light into electricity.
   a. current
   b. converts
   c. conducts

6. The cell must be protected from _____.
   a. dust
   b. light
   c. movement

7. At first, these cells were expensive to make because _____.
   a. the chemical preparation of silicon was expensive
   b. silicon is expensive and hard to find
   c. it is hard to keep dirt off the cells

8. Most of today's air pollution comes from _____.
   a. automobiles
   b. burning fossil fuels
   c. factories

e Comprehension Questions

1. Why do we need a new way to produce energy?
2. Describe a photovoltaic cell.
3. Give three advantages of photovoltaic cells over fossil fuels.
4. In what part of the cell is the electric current created?
5. What does *solid-state* mean?
6. What happens when a photovoltaic cell gets dusty?
7. Why was energy from photovoltaic cells expensive in the beginning?
8. How can these cells help developing countries?
9. Why are photovoltaic cells so important in the space program?

f Main Idea

1. Which sentence is the main idea of paragraph 1 (lines 1–10)?
2. Write a sentence for the main idea of paragraph 2 (lines 11–19).
3. Write the main idea of paragraph 6 (lines 34–40).
4. What is the main idea of paragraph 9 (lines 57–66)?

g Scanning

1. Name a material in the reading that does not conduct electricity.
2. Name a material in the reading that is made mostly of silicon.
3. Name three fossil fuels.

h Two-Word Verbs

Learn these two-word verbs and then fill in the blanks with the right words. Use the correct verb form.

get in   = arrive (for example, a bus or plane)
bring up = raise (for example, children)
show up = appear
stand by = wait at a certain place (for example, for a seat on an airplane when you do not have a reservation)
leave out = skip; forget to include (something)

1. When Ali did his homework, he _____ the third exercise. He forgot to do it.
2. What time does the train from Paris _____?
3. The airline said there were no seats available on this flight, but if someone doesn't _____, I can have that person's seat. I have to _____ until everyone has boarded.
4. Mary was born on a farm, but she was _____ in a small town.

i Missing Words

Fill in the blanks with any word that fits in the sentence.

1. _____ populations increase and countries industrialize, _____ world's demand _____ energy increases.
2. This cell _____ already _____ important source _____ energy.
3. _____ you ever reach _____ open _____ door _____ a store _____ hotel _____ see it open _____ itself?
4. This program could _____ exist _____ the energy produced _____ photovoltaic cells.

5. It has transparent metallic film _____ the top. _____ this is _____ layer of silicon.

6. The sunlight falls _____ the boundary _____ the two different types _____ semiconductors, _____ silicon _____ the metal base.

7. One advantage _____ the photovoltaic cell is that it is solid-state; _____ is, _____ are no moving parts.

8. Since there _____ no moving parts to break _____, the cell _____ last _____ long time _____ it is protected _____ damage.

9. If _____ top of _____ cell _____ dusty, less _____ enters, _____ the cell _____ work as efficiently _____ it should.

j Word Forms

A common use of adjectives is in sentences of this form:

It is + adjective _____.

There are two sentence patterns:

It is necessary *to memorize irregular verbs.*
It is beautiful *to walk by the ocean on a moonlit night.*
It is important *that you fill out these papers immediately.*
It is wonderful *that you won first place in the competition.*

Choose a word form from the chart for each sentence below. Use the right verb forms and singular or plural nouns.

	Verb	Noun	Adjective	Adverb
1.	trap	trap / trapper	trapped	
2.	alternate	alternate / alternative	alternate / alternative	alternately / alternatively
3.	occur	occurrence		
4.	bound	boundary	bound	
5.	theorize	theory	theoretical	theoretically
6.		efficiency	(in)efficient	(in)efficiently
7.		reasonableness	(un)reasonable	(un)reasonably
8.	exhaust	exhaustion	exhausted / (in)exhaustible	(in)exhaustibly
9.		transparency	transparent	transparently
10.	convert	conversion	convertible	

1. When an animal is _____, it can't get away.
2. There is no _____ to our plan. We can find no _____ plan.
3. There were three _____ of breakdowns at the electric power station.
4. Norway is _____ by Sweden, Finland, Russia, the Atlantic Ocean, and the North Sea.
5. Scientists _____ about the center of the Earth, but they can't know for sure.
6. It is _____ to write by hand instead of using a computer.
7. It is _____ to expect a student to memorize fifty new words a day.
8. Scott and his men became _____ on their journey back from the South Pole.
9. _____ is a characteristic of water and glass.
10. Missionaries try to _____ people to their religion.

Lesson 4: Photovoltaic Cells: Energy Source of the Future

k Finding the Reason

Write the reason for each statement.

Statement	Reason
1. The entrance door at a hotel opens by itself.	
2. Electricity can pass through water.	
3. The first photovoltaic cells were very expensive.	
4. These cells can help developing countries.	
5. Energy from the sun is inexhaustible.	
6. The photovoltaic cell can't break down.	
7. The photovoltaic cell might work inefficiently.	

 ## l Guided Writing

Write one of these two short compositions.

1. What are some of the advantages of solar energy over energy made from fossil fuels?
2. What are some of the disadvantages of solar energy?

lesson
5

Biological Clocks

© Bruce Rowell/Masterfile

Before You Read

1. How do you feel when you have to get up much earlier than usual?

2. Do you feel best early in the morning, in the middle of the day, in the afternoon, at sunset, or late at night?

3. If you take a long trip on an airplane, do you have trouble getting used to the time change?

Context Clues

*The words in **bold** print are from this lesson. Use context clues to guess the meaning of each word.*

1. In the **temperate** zones of the Earth, trees lose their leaves in the fall. In the spring, leaves and flowers begin growing again as the days lengthen.

2. When winter comes, some birds **migrate** to a region with a warmer climate.

3. To be comfortable on an airplane, wear **loose** clothing and take your shoes off while you are in your seat.

4. On the fourth day before taking a long trip by airplane, eat three big meals. Then, on the third day, **fast** for the whole day.

5   Biological Clocks

If you have ever flown across several time zones, you have experienced **jet lag.** You arrived in a new time zone, but your body was still living on the time in the old zone. You were **wide awake** and ready for dinner in
5   the middle of the night, and you wanted to sleep all day.

People suffer from jet lag because all living things have a **biological** clock. Plants and animals are all in
<u>rhythm</u> with the natural divisions of time—day and   a regular beat
night and the seasons.

10   At sunrise, plants open their leaves and begin producing food. At night, they rest. In the **temperate** zones of the Earth, trees lose their leaves in the fall as the days grow shorter and there is less sunlight. In the spring, leaves and flowers begin growing again as
15   the days lengthen.

Rain sets the rhythm of desert plants. Plants in the desert may appear dead for months or even years, but when it begins to rain, the plants seem to come to life

overnight. The leaves turn green, and flowers appear.
20 The plants produce seeds quickly, before the rain
stops. These seeds may lie on the ground for years
before rain starts the cycle of growth again. The plants'
biological clock gives the **signal** for these things
to happen.

25   At **<u>dawn</u>**, most birds wake up and start singing.   sunrise
When the sun goes down, they go to sleep. When spring
arrives, they start looking for a mate. When winter
comes, some birds **migrate** to a region with a warmer
climate. Their biological clocks tell them that it is time to
30 do all of these things.

Animals that live near the sea and depend on both
the land and water for their food have their biological
clocks set with the **tides.** When the tide goes out,
they know that it is time to search for the food that the
35 sea left behind.

Some insects seem to set their **alarm** clocks to wake
them up at night. They stay out all night looking for
food, and then they sleep during the day. Honeybees
have a very strong sense of time. They can tell by the
40 position of the sun exactly when their favorite
flowers open.

Some French scientists did an experiment with
honeybees. They put out sugar water every morning at
10:00 and at noon, and the bees came to drink the
45 water at exactly the right time. Then the scientists put
the sugar water in a room that was brightly lit
twenty-four hours a day. They started putting the
sugar water out at 8:00 p.m. It took the bees a week to
find it at the different hour, but from then on, they
50 came to eat in the evening instead of in the morning.
Later, the scientists took the honeybees to New York.
The bees came for the food at the time their bodies told
them, only it was 3:00 p.m. New York time. Their
bodies were still on Paris time.

55   Humans, like other animals, have a biological clock
that tells them when to sleep and eat. It causes other
changes too. Blood pressure is lower at night, the
heartbeat is slower, and the body temperature is a little

211

lower. We even go through several levels of sleep, cycles
60 of deep and light sleep.

Other events occur in cycles too. More babies are
born between midnight and dawn than at any other
time. More natural deaths occur at night, but more heart
attacks happen early in the morning. Most deaths from
65 diseases in hospitals occur between midnight and
6:00 a.m. Some police say that there are more violent
crimes and traffic accidents when there is a full moon.

The honeybees in the experiment reset their
biological clock for different feeding hours. Humans do
70 this too. People who work at night learn to sleep during
the day and eat at night. Students who fly halfway
across the world to study in another country get used to
the new time zone after a few days. When they go
home, they change back again. Our bodies are
75 controlled by a biological clock, but we can learn to
reset it to a different time.

How to <u>**Lessen**</u> Jet Lag
make less; decrease

1. Try not to become exhausted before you leave. Get
80   plenty of sleep, and leave enough time to get to the
    airport and check in without having to hurry.
2. Wear <u>**loose**</u> clothing and take your shoes off while   not tight
    you are in your seat.
3. Walk around the plane and move around in your seat.
85 4. Figure out breakfast time in the time zone you are
    flying to. Four days before your flight, start a **feast**
    (eating a lot) and **fast** (eating nothing or very little)
    schedule. On the fourth day before you fly, eat three
    heavy meals. If you drink coffee, tea, or cola drinks
90   that contain **caffeine,** have them only between
    3:00 and 5:00 p.m. On the third day before your
    flight, eat very lightly—salads, light soups, fruits,
    and juices. Again, have drinks with caffeine only
    between 3:00 and 5:00 p.m. On the next to the last
95   day before you leave, feast again. On the day before
    you leave, fast. If you are flying west, drink
    caffeinated drinks in the morning; if you are going
    east, drink them between 6:00 and 11:00 p.m.

212

5. On the day you leave, have your first meal at the
100   time people in the new time zone eat breakfast.
       If the flight is long, sleep on the plane until the new
       breakfast time, and don't drink any alcohol. When
       you wake up, have a big meal. Stay awake and
       active, and eat at the new time zone hours.

a Vocabulary

signal	active	wide awake	attack
alarm	biology	rhythm	jet lag
temperate	migrate	heartbeat	fast

1. Countries with _____ climates have four different seasons.
2. The science and study of life is called _____.
3. You should drive a car only when you are _____.
4. Some people like to listen to the _____ of the falling rain.
5. Many people _____ for religious reasons.
6. When the fire _____ sounded, everyone left the building.
7. Doctors listen to a person's _____ through a stethoscope to see if there are any irregularities.
8. Larger animals will often _____ smaller animals.
9. Pilots don't usually suffer from _____ because they never stay in the new time zone very long.

b Vocabulary

rhythm	dawn	temperate	tides
feast	lessens	migrate	signal
active	caffeine	loose	attack

1. Chocolate, tea, coffee, and cola drinks contain _____.
2. The police officer gave a _____ for the cars to stop.
3. Some birds _____ to a warmer climate in the winter.
4. The villagers prepared a _____ to entertain the visiting government officials.
5. There are high and low _____ in the ocean twice a day.
6. The sun rises at _____.
7. _____ is the opposite of *tight*.
8. A different diet _____ the effects of jet lag.
9. People who are _____ seem to live longer than people who don't get much exercise.

c Vocabulary Review

astonishing	ranges	tools	senses
cope	projects	rolls	layers
flood	colony	mild	surface

1. If you don't like cold winters, you should move to a _____ climate.
2. A carpenter cannot work without _____.
3. Your biological clock has an _____ effect on your body.
4. In cold climates, it makes sense to wear several _____ of clothing.
5. Dust on the _____ of a photovoltaic cell makes it work inefficiently.
6. Hearing is one of the five _____.
7. A ball or other round object _____.
8. The temperature here _____ from 30°F to 90°F.

214

9. Biospheres are special _____ at some environmental research laboratories.
10. It's difficult to _____ when several bad things happen at the same time.

d True/False/Not Enough Information

_____ 1. Jet lag occurs when your body is in one time zone but your biological clock is in another.

_____ 2. Plants begin producing nutrients when the sun rises.

_____ 3. Plants in Iceland and Greenland can produce nutrients twenty-four hours a day during the summer.

_____ 4. A biological clock gives birds the signal that it is time to migrate.

_____ 5. Animals that live near the sea search for food at night when it is safer.

_____ 6. The honeybees in the experiment reset their biological clocks.

_____ 7. After a few days, the bees probably changed their biological clocks to New York time.

_____ 8. The human biological clock affects many parts of the body.

_____ 9. Humans cannot change their biological clocks once they are set, but bees can.

_____ 10. You can decrease the effects of jet lag.

e Comprehension Questions

1. What makes desert plants produce seeds?
2. Why do birds wake at dawn?
3. How do honeybees know when a flower opens?
4. Why do honeybees want to know when a flower opens?
5. What is the time difference between New York and Paris?
6. Why should you wear loose clothing on a long flight?
7. Why should you have breakfast at breakfast time in the new time zone on the day you leave?

f | Main Idea

Copy or write a sentence for the main idea of each of these paragraphs.

1. Paragraph 4 (lines 16–24)
2. Paragraph 8 (lines 42–54)
3. Paragraph 9 (lines 55–60)
4. Paragraph 11 (lines 68–76)

g | Word Forms: Adjectives

Both the **-ing** form of the verb (the present participle) and the **-ed** form (the past participle) are used as adjectives. The **-ed** form often shows that the noun received the action, or it describes how a person feels. The **-ing** form often shows some action that the noun took, or it describes an object or possibly a person. However, there are many exceptions.

> David was **bored** because the movie was **boring.**

> Tome is **interested** in stamps. He thinks stamps are **interesting.**

> Mary is an **interesting** person because she can talk about a lot of different things.

Put the right participle form of the verb in parentheses in each sentence.

1. Climbing a mountain is (exhaust) _____ work.
2. Al was (exhaust) _____ after the soccer game.
3. Mr. Davis is a very (demand) _____ teacher. He makes the students work hard and do their best.
4. There are two kinds of electric current, direct and (alternate) _____.
5. The (trap) _____ animal couldn't escape.
6. A (damage) _____ car needs to be fixed.
7. Children like to play (guess) _____ games.
8. The breakup of their marriage was a (surprise) _____ event.
9. American football is a (complicate) _____ game.
10. Being in an airplane crash is a (terrify) _____ experience.

h Word Forms: Semi-

Semi- is a prefix that means *half* or *partly*. These are some common words with this prefix:

semicircle
semicolon (;)
semitransparent
semifinal (describing the next-to-last round in sports competitions); semifinalist
semitropical (Hawaii is semitropical, but it is not in the tropics.)
semiyearly (twice a year)
semiretired
semiprivate (describing a hospital room with beds for two or three patients)
semiprecious

Use five of these words in interesting sentences.

 ## i Prepositions

Put the right preposition in each blank.

1. If you have ever flown _____ several time zones, you have experienced jet lag.
2. You arrived _____ a new time zone, but your body was still living _____ the time _____ the old zone.
3. You were wide awake and ready _____ dinner _____ the middle _____ the night.
4. Plants and animals are all _____ rhythm _____ the natural divisions _____ time.
5. _____ the temperate zones _____ the Earth, trees lose their leaves _____ the fall as the days grow shorter.
6. Plants _____ the desert may appear dead _____ months or even years.
7. Some animals depend _____ the sea for their food.
8. Some insects wake up _____ night.

9. Honeybees can tell _____ the position _____ the sun exactly when their favorite flowers open.

10. Scientists put out sugar water every morning _____ 10:00 and _____ noon.

j Connecting Words

*Use **since, when, until,** or **even though** to connect a sentence from the first column with one from the second column.*

1. The bees were ready to eat their evening meal.
2. It has been snowing.
3. Chris stopped drinking coffee in the evening.
4. Birds start singing.
5. A photovoltaic cell is efficient.

a. It was only 3:00 p.m. in New York.
b. It kept her awake.
c. It becomes dusty.
d. The sun went down.
e. The sun rises.

k Sequence

Put these sentences about the French experiment in the right order.

_____ a. The scientists took the bees to New York.

_____ b. Some French scientists did an experiment.

_____ c. They put the sugar water out at 8:00 p.m.

_____ d. They put the sugar water out at 10:00 a.m. and at noon.

_____ e. The bees looked for food at 3:00 p.m. New York time.

_____ f. The bees took a week to find the food at a different time.

_____ g. The bees came every evening at 8:00 p.m.

■ Guided Writing

Write one of these two short compositions.

1. What does *biological clock* mean? Give examples.
2. Describe a time when you experienced jet lag.

Video Highlights

a Before You Watch

1. Use your own knowledge and a world map to discuss these questions.
    a. Which hemisphere of the Earth do you live in, the Northern Hemisphere or the Southern Hemisphere?
    b. Is it safe or dangerous to spend a lot of time in direct sunlight? Why?
    c. What are some of the things people use that cause damage to the Earth's atmosphere?
2. The paragraph below describes a chemical process that takes place in the Earth's atmosphere. Use the diagram to fill in the missing words.

   The ozone layer is part of the atmosphere that surrounds the Earth. It is made up of ozone (O_3) molecules, which form a protective shield against the _____ rays of the sun. Some of the things people use every day are causing serious damage to the ozone layer. For example, chemicals used for air conditioning and refrigerators release harmful chlorine (Cl) molecules into the atmosphere. The chlorine molecules react with the _____ molecules to break them down. This process gradually eats up the ozone layer.

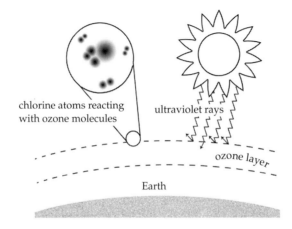

chlorine atoms reacting with ozone molecules

ultraviolet rays

ozone layer

Earth

b   As You Watch

According to the scientists in the video, which of the following is the main cause of damage to the ozone layer?

☐ flights over the Northern Hemisphere
☐ ultraviolet rays from the sun
☐ widespread use of manmade chemicals

c   After You Watch

1. Start from the bottom of this "ladder." Each cause leads to an effect, which in turn causes another effect. Fill in the missing words.
2. Using the cause and effect ladder you completed, explain to a partner how using certain chemicals can cause harm to all living things.

   Example: When you use chemicals known as CFCs, they release . . .

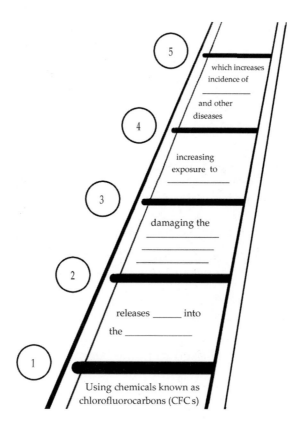

5   which increases incidence of
_____ and other diseases

4   increasing exposure to _____

3   damaging the _____ _____

2   releases _____ into the _____

1   Using chemicals known as chlorofluorocarbons (CFCs)

Activity Page

Chemical Crossword Puzzle

Across

2. Common abbreviation for chlorofluorocarbon
5. Too much of this gas can cause destruction of the rain forest (two words).
8. Silicon is an example of a _____-metallic element.
9. This gas forms a layer that helps protect the Earth from the sun.

Down

1. This element is used in photovoltaic cells.
2. This gas causes damage to the ozone layer.
3. Chemical symbol for #1 down
4. Chemical symbol for #7 down
6. Necessary for all animal life
7. A very strong metal used to make beams for skyscrapers

Doing Dictionary Research

1. Look up the word *geothermal* in your dictionary. How many other words do you see that begin with *geo-*?

ge·og·ra·phy /ʤiˈɑgrəfi/ *n.* **1** the scientific study of the earth's surface, features, climate, people, etc.: *I bought a new atlas for my geography class.* **2** the way parts of a place are positioned within it, (*syn.*) layout: *I can't meet you inside the mall because I don't know the geography of the place, and I might get lost.* *-adj.* **geographic**/ˌʤiəˈgræfɪk/.

ge·ol·o·gy /ʤiˈɑləʤi/ *n.* the scientific study of the earth through its rocks, soil, etc.: *In geology we studied the rocks and deserts of California.* *-n.* **geologist**; *-adj.* **geologic** /ˌʤiəˈlɑʤɪk/.

ge·o·met·ric /ˌʤiəˈmɛtrɪk/ *adj.* with regular shapes and lines: *The mosque's walls are decorated with geometric designs.*

ge·om·e·try /ʤiˈɑmətri/ *n.* the study in mathematics of lines, angles, shapes, etc.: *It is important to study geometry if you want to be an architect.*

ge·o·phys·ics /ˌʤiouˈfɪzɪks/ *n.pl. used with a sing. v.* the study in geology that uses physics to examine the movements and activities of the earth

ge·o·pol·i·tics /ˌʤiouˈpɑlətɪks/ *n.pl. used with a sing. v.* the study of how geography affects the politics of a country

ge·o·ther·mal /ˌʤiouˈθɜrməl/ *adj.* related to heat found deep inside the earth: *The geysers in Yellowstone National Park are geothermal because of hot water coming from inside the earth. See:* geyser.

2. This dictionary page has seven words beginning with *geo-*. Read their definitions and answer the following questions.

   a. How are the meanings of the words *geography, geology, geometric, geophysics,* and *geopolitics* alike?

   b. What do you think the prefix *geo-* means?

3. Look up the words *psychology, microscopic,* and *semiconductor* in your dictionary. Look for other words nearby that have related meanings. Then complete the chart below.

Word	Related Word	Prefix	Meaning
psychology	psychopath psychic	psych-	related to the mind
microscopic			
semiconductor			

Medicine and Health

Early to bed and early to rise makes a man healthy, wealthy, and wise.
—Benjamin Franklin

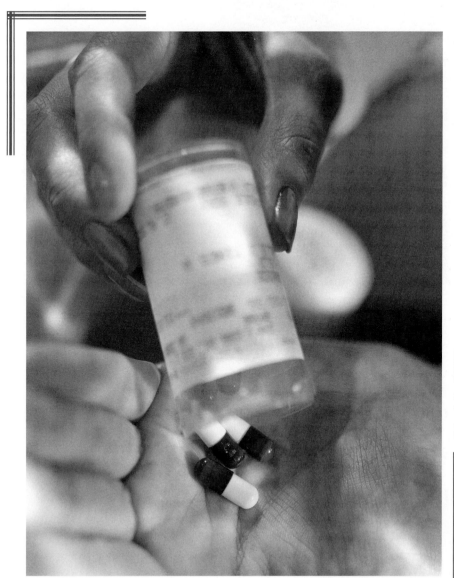

© Royalty-Free/CORBIS

Headaches

lesson
1

© Tom Stewart/CORBIS

Before You Read

1. How often do you have a headache?

2. What causes you to have a headache?

3. How do you treat your headaches?

Context Clues

*The words in **bold** print are from this lesson. Use context clues to guess the meaning of each word.*

1. Sometimes headaches start with a change in **vision**. The person sees wavy lines, black dots, or bright spots in front of the eyes.

2. Some headaches cause **blurred** vision, and you can't read or drive.

3. **Cluster** headaches come in clusters, or groups, for two or three months.

4. If you have a headache and it continues over several days, or keeps **recurring,** it is time to talk to a doctor.

1   **Headaches**

Some little man is inside your head, **pounding** on your brain with a <u>hammer.</u> Beside him, a rock musician is playing a drum. Your head feels as if it is going to explode. You have a **headache,** and you think it will
5 never go away.

hammer

Doctors say that there are several kinds of headaches. Each kind begins in a different place and needs a different treatment. One kind of headache starts in the **arteries** in the head. The arteries <u>swell</u> and send **pain**
10 signals to the brain. Sometimes these headaches start with a change in <u>vision.</u> The person sees wavy lines, black dots, or bright spots in front of the eyes. This is a **warning** that a headache is coming. The headache occurs on only one side of the head. Vision is **blurred,** and the
15 person may **vomit** from the pain. These headaches, which are called **migraine** headaches, are more frequent in women than in men. Sleep is the best cure for them.

get larger

ability to see; sight

227

Cluster headaches, which also start in the arteries, are called cluster headaches because they come in clusters, or groups, for two or three months. Then there are no more for several months or even years. A cluster headache lasts up to two hours and then goes away. At the beginning of the headache, the eyes are red and watery. There is a **steady** pain in the head. When the pain finally goes away, the head is **sore.** Men have more cluster headaches than women do.

continuing
painful

The muscle headache, which starts in the muscles in the neck or **forehead,** is caused by **tension.** A person works too hard, is nervous about something, or has problems at work, at school, or at home. The neck and head muscles become tense, and the headache starts. A muscle headache usually starts in the morning and gets worse as the hours pass. There is a steady pain, pressure, and a bursting feeling. Usually **aspirin** doesn't help a muscle headache very much.

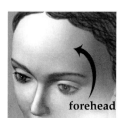
forehead

How do doctors treat headaches? If a person has frequent headaches, the doctor first has to decide what kind they are. Medicine can help, but there are other ways to treat them.

The doctor asks the patient to **analyze** his or her daily living patterns. A change in diet or an increase in exercise might stop the headaches. If the **patient** realizes that difficulties at home, at work, or at school are causing the tension, it might be possible to make **lifestyle** changes and decrease these problems. Psychological problems and even medicine for another **physical** problem can cause headaches. The doctor has to discuss and analyze all these patterns in the patient's life. A headache can also be a signal of a more serious problem.

of the body

Everyone has headaches from time to time. In the United States alone, up to 50 million people each year go to the doctor because of headaches. If you have a headache and it continues over several days, or keeps **recurring,** it is time to talk to a doctor. There is no magic cure for headaches, but recent research allows doctors to control most of them.

occurring again

a Vocabulary

pounded	swells	lifestyle	migraine
clusters	sore	forehead	aspirin
recur	analyze	pain	hammer

1. To _____ means to *happen again*.

2. If your arm is _____, it hurts. You have a _____ in your arm.

3. The _____ is the top part of the face.

4. _____ helps some kinds of headaches.

5. When we went to our friend's apartment, we knocked and then _____ on the door, but no one answered.

6. One kind of headache is called a _____.

7. A _____ is one kind of tool.

8. When you put air in a bicycle tire, the tire _____ until it fits the wheel exactly.

9. After the TOEFL test, the students gathered in small _____ to talk about it.

10. Even though he is very rich, his _____ is just like an ordinary person's.

11. Before you do anything, you should _____ the situation carefully.

b Vocabulary

ache	warned	blurred	arteries
vomit	hammer	physical	swell
steady	patients	vision	tense

1. When you are sick and in pain, your stomach may protest and make you _____.

2. The teacher _____ the children that they had to behave or there would be no party.

3. Sick people in the hospital are called _____.

4. While Pat was swimming, she got water in her eye. Everything looked _____ to her.

5. Students often feel _____ before an important exam.

6. A complete _____ examination is necessary for anyone entering the army.

7. The farmers were happy when a _____ rain continued all night.

8. _____ carry blood from the heart to the rest of the body.

9. You may get a stomach _____ if you eat too much.

10. People with poor _____ wear glasses or contact lenses.

c Vocabulary Review: Antonyms

Match the opposites.

_____	1. fiction	a.	point
_____	2. scatter	b.	import
_____	3. active	c.	nonfiction
_____	4. reluctant	d.	ordinary
_____	5. unique	e.	microscope
_____	6. last	f.	run out
_____	7. export	g.	gather
_____	8. loose	h.	increase
_____	9. fast	i.	inactive
_____	10. lessen	j.	eager
		k.	feast
		l.	tight

d Multiple Choice

1. When someone sees black dots or wavy lines, this is a change in _____.
   a. blurring
   b. clusters
   c. vision

2. A migraine headache causes _____.
   a. blurred vision
   b. red and watery eyes
   c. a bursting feeling

3. _____ is the best cure for migraines.
   a. Sleep
   b. Aspirin
   c. Arteries

4. _____ have more headaches that leave the head sore.
   a. Women
   b. Men
   c. Older people

5. A _____ headache starts in the morning and gets worse.
   a. migraine
   b. cluster
   c. muscle

6. Tension causes a _____ headache.
   a. migraine
   b. cluster
   c. muscle

7. Medicine is _____ headaches.
   a. the best treatment for
   b. not usually helpful for
   c. one way to treat

8. A change in a patient's lifestyle can _____.
   a. help cure headaches
   b. cause headaches
   c. both a and b

e Comprehension Questions

1. Describe a migraine headache.
2. Describe a cluster headache.
3. Describe a muscle headache.
4. Which kind of headache affects more women than men?

5. What are some things that can cause a muscle headache?
6. If you have a headache, will aspirin help?
7. Why does a doctor analyze the life patterns of a headache patient?
8. How many people each year in the United States go to a doctor for headaches?

 f Main Idea

Write the main idea of each of these paragraphs.

1. Paragraph 2 (lines 6–17)
2. Paragraph 3 (lines 18–26)
3. Paragraph 7 (lines 51–57)

 g Word Forms

Choose a word form from the chart for each sentence below. Use the right verb forms and singular or plural nouns.

	Verb	Noun	Adjective	Adverb
1.	press	pressure		
2.		reluctance	reluctant	reluctantly
3.	migrate	migration	migrant	
4.	lessen	least	less	
5.	warn	warning		
6.	pain	pain	painful / painless	painfully / painlessly
7.	swell	swelling	swollen	
8.	recur	recurrence	recurrent	recurrently
9.	tense	tension	tense	tensely
10.	prove	proof	proven	

1. Mr. Johnson has high blood _____. He has to take medicine every day.
2. She _____ agreed to play basketball.
3. Scientists study the _____ of birds.
4. The pain of some headaches is _____ by aspirin.
5. A fire alarm is a _____ to leave the building.
6. A broken arm is _____.
7. Dan hurt his hand, and now it is _____.
8. After the fifth _____ of a bad headache, Mark went to a doctor.
9. _____ causes muscle headaches.
10. Scientists have _____ that photovoltaic cells convert sunlight directly into energy. This was _____ some years ago.

h Scanning

Scan the text to assign each of these sentences to the correct column. In the correct column, write the number of the line in the text where you found the idea.

	Migraine	Cluster	Muscle
a. They come in groups.			
b. It starts in the neck or forehead.			
c. It is caused by tension.			
d. There is a change in vision.			
e. There may not be any for several years.			
f. Aspirin doesn't help.			
g. Sleep helps.			
h. It occurs on only one side of the head.			
i. It lasts for two hours or less.			
j. Problems at work can cause it.			

Noun Substitutes

What do these words stand for?

1. page 227 line 2   **him**   _____

2. page 227 line 3   **it**   _____

3. page 227 line 12   **this**   _____

4. page 227 line 17   **them**   _____

5. page 228 line 18   **which**   _____

6. page 228 line 27   **which**   _____

7. page 228 lines 40   **his or her**   _____

8. page 228 line 57   **them**   _____

Articles

Put articles in the blanks if they are necessary.

1. Beside him, _____ rock musician is playing _____ drum.

2. Each kind begins in _____ different place and needs _____ different treatment.

3. One kind of headache starts in _____ arteries in _____ head.

4. _____ arteries swell and send _____ pain signals to _____ brain.

5. Sometimes these headaches start with a change in _____ vision.

6. _____ person sees _____ wavy lines, _____ black dots, or _____ bright spots in front of _____ eyes.

7. This is _____ warning that _____ headache is coming.

8. _____ headache occurs on only one side of _____ head.

9. _____ vision is blurred, and _____ person may vomit from _____ pain.

10. _____ sleep is _____ best cure for them.

k Verb + Adjective

Adjectives usually follow these verbs: **be, feel, become, seem, act, appear, look, smell, taste.**

She is sick.	He appears tired.
She feels sick.	He looks tired.
She became sick a week ago.	It smells good.
He seems tired.	It tastes good.
He acts tired.	

Use each verb in an interesting sentence.

 ## l Guided Writing

Write one of these two short compositions.

1. Describe the different kinds of headaches.
2. Discuss ways to treat and cure headaches.

lesson
2

Sleep and Dreams

© H. Armstrong Roberts/CORBIS

Before You Read

1. How often do you dream?

2. Do you walk in your sleep?

3. Why do you think we dream?

Context Clues

*The words in **bold** print are from this lesson. Use context clues to guess the meaning of each word.*

1. Scientists have learned **a great deal** by studying people as they sleep, but there is still much that they don't understand.

2. Your brain never really sleeps. It is never actually **blank.**

3. During a dream, the brain may **concentrate** on a problem and look for different solutions.

4. Some people grind their teeth while they sleep. They wake up with a sore **jaw** or a headache.

5. Lots of people take sleeping pills, but these are dangerous because they can be **addictive**. If you take them for several weeks, it is hard to stop taking them.

2 Sleep and Dreams

Sleep is very important to humans; the average person spends 220,000 hours of his or her lifetime sleeping. Doctors and scientists have learned **a great deal** in the last thirty years by studying people as they

a lot

5 sleep, but there is still much that they don't understand.
Scientists study the body characteristics that change during sleep, such as body temperature, brain waves, blood pressure, breathing, and heartbeat. They also study rapid eye movement (REM). These scientists have
10 learned that there is a kind of sleep with REM and another kind with no rapid eye movement (NREM).
NREM is divided into three **stages.** In stage one, when you start to go to sleep, you have a pleasant floating feeling. A sudden noise can wake you up. In
15 stage two, you sleep more deeply, and a noise will

237

probably not wake you. In stage three, which you reach in less than thirty minutes, the brain waves are less active and stretched out. Then, within another half hour, you reach REM sleep. This stage might last an hour and
20 a half and is the time when you dream. For the rest of the night, REM and NREM sleep alternate.

Sleep is a biological need, but your brain never really sleeps. It is never actually **blank**. The things that were on your mind during the day are still there at night. They
25 appear as dreams. At times, people believed that dreams had magical powers or that they could tell the future.

sweating

Sometimes dreams are terrifying, but they are usually a collection of scattered, <u>**confused**</u> thoughts. If you dream about something that is worrying you, you may wake up
30 exhausted, <u>**sweating,**</u> and with a rapid heartbeat. Dreams can have positive effects on our lives. During a dream, the brain may <u>**concentrate**</u> on a problem and look for different solutions. Also, people who dream during a good night's sleep are more likely to remember newly learned skills. In
35 other words, you learn better if you dream.

mixed up

think hard

Researchers say that normal people may have four or five REM <u>**periods**</u> of dreaming a night. The first one may begin only a half hour after they fall asleep. Each period of dreaming is a little longer, the final one lasting up to
40 an hour. Dreams also become more <u>**intense**</u> as the night continues. <u>**Nightmares**</u> usually occur toward dawn.

lengths of time

very strong
bad dreams

Certain people can control some of their dreams and make sure they have a happy ending. Some people get **relief** from bad dreams by writing them down and then
45 changing the negative stories or thoughts into positive ones on paper. Then they study the paper before they go to sleep again.

Sleepwalking is most common among children. They usually grow out of it by the time they become
50 <u>**adolescents.**</u> Children don't remember that they were walking in their sleep, and they don't usually wake up if the parent leads them back to bed.

teenagers

Some people have a **habit** of grinding their teeth while they sleep. They wake up with a sore **jaw** or a
55 headache, and they can also damage their teeth.

238

Researchers don't know why people talk, walk, or grind their teeth while they are asleep.

There are lots of jokes about **snoring**, but it isn't really funny. People snore because they have trouble
60 breathing while they are asleep. Some snorers have a condition called sleep apnea. They stop breathing up to thirty or forty times an hour because the throat muscles relax too much and **block** the airway. Then they breathe in some air and start snoring. This is a dangerous
65 condition because, if the brain is without oxygen for four minutes, there will be **permanent** brain damage.   lasting forever
Sleep apnea can also cause irregular heartbeats, high blood pressure, and a general lack of energy.

Most people need from 7½ to 8½ hours of sleep a
70 night, but this varies with the individual. Babies sleep eighteen hours, and old people need less sleep than younger people. If someone continually sleeps longer than normal for no **apparent** reason, there may be   obvious; adjective
something physically or psychologically wrong.   for *appear*

75 What should you do if you have trouble sleeping? Lots of people take sleeping pills, but these are dangerous because they can be **addictive**. If you take them for several weeks, it is hard to stop taking them.

Doctors say the best thing is to try to relax and to
80 avoid bad habits. Caffeine keeps people awake, so don't drink anything with caffeine in the evening. Smoking and alcohol can also keep you awake. You may have trouble sleeping if you have a heavy meal just before you go to bed.

85 You may also have trouble sleeping if you have something on your mind. Try to relax. If you are thinking about a problem or about something exciting that is going to happen the next day, get up and write about it. That will help take it off your mind. You can also get up and
90 read or watch television. Be sure to choose a book or show that is not too exciting, or you may get so interested that you won't want to go to sleep even when you feel sleepy.

Sleep is important to humans. We spend a third of our lives sleeping, so we need to understand everything
95 we can about sleep. Sweet dreams!

a Vocabulary

stage	periods	snore	habit
blank	nightmare	confused	block
a great deal	relief	sweat	concentrate

1. It is hard to _____ on your homework if your roommate is playing loud music.
2. The instructor asked everyone to take out a _____ piece of paper.
3. In the first _____ of a volcanic eruption, the volcano sends out smoke.
4. A _____ is a bad dream.
5. Do you _____ loudly when you sleep?
6. The school day is divided into several _____, one for each class.
7. It's a _____ when the sun comes out after a bad storm.
8. Sylvia has a _____ of having a cup of coffee as soon as she gets home from work.
9. Hard exercise makes you _____.
10. A Mercedes-Benz is a car that costs _____ of money.

b Vocabulary

confused	concentrate	intense	adolescents
jaws	blank	apparently	addictive
habit	block	permanently	relieve

1. The teeth are in the upper and lower _____.
2. The _____ summer heat of the Arabian Desert can be very dangerous if you're not careful.
3. A car accident can _____ traffic on a highway.
4. David was _____ about the date, so he missed the meeting.
5. It's difficult to _____ when you are trying to do two things at the same time.

6. An immigrant plans to stay in a new country _____.

7. The professor seems to be very busy. _____, he has a lot of work to do.

8. _____ are not children, but they are not grown up either.

9. Smoking is _____, so it's better not to even start smoking.

c Vocabulary Review: Definitions

Match the words with the definitions.

_____ 1. melt		a.	middle
_____ 2. mid-		b.	soreness
_____ 3. strip		c.	fingerprint
_____ 4. export		d.	reasonable
_____ 5. pain		e.	with no moving parts
_____ 6. inexhaustible		f.	change from a solid to a liquid
_____ 7. solid-state		g.	able to be seen through
_____ 8. source		h.	because
_____ 9. transparent		i.	long, thin piece
_____ 10. boundary		j.	place
_____ 11. since		k.	sell to other countries
_____ 12. position		l.	not able to be used up
_____ 13. astonishing		m.	place something comes from
		n.	border
		o.	surprising

d True/False/Not Enough Information

_____ 1. We spend about a third of our lives sleeping.

_____ 2. Researchers now understand nearly everything about sleep.

_____ 3. NREM sleep comes before the REM stage.

_____ 4. After the three stages of NREM, REM lasts the rest of the night.

_____ 5. Dreams occur during the REM stage, but the brain is normally blank the rest of the time.

_____ 6. A dream about an unhappy event can change your heartbeat.

_____ 7. Nightmares occur early, when dreams are short.

_____ 8. Sleep apnea is the cause of some snoring.

_____ 9. Five or six hours of sleep is enough for some people.

_____ 10. The best thing to do when you have trouble sleeping is to take sleeping pills.

Comprehension Questions

1. How have researchers learned about sleep?
2. What does _REM_ mean?
3. How do dreams change as the sleep period continues?
4. Can sleepwalking be dangerous? Give a reason for your answer.
5. Why do some people grind their teeth while they sleep?
6. How can sleep apnea cause brain damage?
7. Name three things that can keep you awake.
8. How does a problem keep you from sleeping?

Main Idea

Find or write a sentence for the main idea of each of these paragraphs.

1. Paragraph 3 (lines 12–21)
2. Paragraph 4 (lines 22–26)
3. Paragraph 6 (lines 36–41)
4. Paragraph 11 (lines 69–74)

Scanning

Write short answers for these questions and the line numbers on which you found the answers.

1. In what stage of NREM sleep can a sudden noise wake you up?
2. Why do people snore?
3. Why is it a bad idea to take sleeping pills?
4. How many REM periods of dreaming do people normally have?
5. What did some people believe about dreams?
6. What should you do if you can't sleep because you are thinking about an exciting event the next day?
7. Is it possible to control dreams?
8. How many hours a day do babies sleep?

h Connecting Words

*Use **before, after, although,** or **since** to connect a sentence from the first column with one in the second.*

1. Scientists don't know everything about sleep.
2. We shouldn't laugh about snoring.
3. Don't eat a heavy meal.
4. Go to bed and get up at about the same time.
5. The REM stage begins.

a. You go to bed.
b. It isn't really funny.
c. The NREM stage begins.
d. They have learned a lot in the last thirty years.
e. This sets a rhythm in your life.

i Missing Words

Write any word that is correct in each blank.

1. Sleep is very important _____ humans; _____ average person spends 220,000 hours of his or her lifetime sleeping.
2. They have learned _____ great deal _____ studying people as they sleep.
3. Scientists study _____ body characteristics that change _____ sleep.
4. NREM _____ divided _____ three stages.
5. You reach stage three _____ less _____ thirty minutes.
6. Sleep is _____ biological need, _____ your brain never really sleeps.
7. _____ things that were _____ your mind during _____ day are still there _____ night.
8. _____ times, people believed _____ dreams had magical powers _____ that they could tell _____ future.
9. Dreams can have _____ positive effects _____ our lives.

j Word Forms

Choose a word form from the chart for each sentence below. Use the right verb forms and singular or plural nouns.

	Verb	Noun	Adjective	Adverb
1.	convert	conversion		
2.		habit	habitual	habitually
3.	concentrate	concentration	concentrated	
4.	confuse	confusion	confused	
5.		intensity	intense	intensely
6.		adolescence	adolescent	
7.	breathe	breath breathing	breathless	breathlessly
8.		permanence	permanent	permanently
9.	loosen	looseness	loose	loosely
10.	(dis)appear	(dis)appearance	apparent	apparently

1. You can _____ your money into dollars at the bank.
2. The present tense is used for _____ actions.
3. a. Great _____ is necessary for the game of chess.
   b. Most of Australia's population is _____ on the east coast.
4. There was a lot of _____ about the new class schedule, but now it is all cleared up and things are going smoothly. At first, the students were _____.
5. Susan feels everything very _____.
6. _____ is a difficult time for some young Americans and their parents.
7. Tom spoke _____ because he was so excited.

8. Nora married a German and is going to live _____ in Germany.

9. Carol _____ her belt because it was too tight.

10. The plane got in an hour ago, but Mohammed didn't come through the gate. _____, he wasn't on it.

k Guided Writing

Write one of these two short compositions. Paraphrase the information as much as possible.

1. When and why do we dream?
2. If a person has trouble sleeping, what can he or she do about it?

lesson
3

Health Care
and Epidemics

Alan Hindle/CORBIS

Before You Read

1. When you are sick, do you take medicine? Why?

2. How can people prevent disease?

3. Have you ever been in a place that was having an epidemic? What did the people do about it?

Context Clues

*The words in **bold** print are from this lesson. Use context clues to guess the meaning of each word.*

1. Some diseases are caused by **viruses.** Viruses are even smaller than bacteria, and they cause different kinds of diseases.

2. People can be **cruel** to victims of disease. Sometimes they take away their jobs, throw them out of their apartments, and refuse them transportation.

3. Some diseases spread when people touch the same dishes, towels, and furniture. You can even **pick up** a disease when you touch things in public buildings.

4. One disease that causes frequent, worldwide epidemics is **influenza,** or flu for short. The symptoms of influenza include a headache and sometimes a runny nose.

5. About half of all flu patients have a high body temperature, called a **fever.**

3   Health Care and Epidemics

Everyone suffers from disease at some time or another. However, millions of people around the world do not have good health care. Sometimes they have no money to pay for medical treatment. Sometimes they
5 have money, but there is no doctor. Sometimes the doctor does not know how to treat the disease, and sometimes there is no treatment. Some people are afraid of doctors. When these conditions are present in large population centers, **epidemics** can start.
10   Epidemics can change history. Exploration and wars cause different groups of people to come into contact with

each other. They carry strange diseases to each other. For example, when the Europeans first came to North and South America, they brought diseases with them that
15 killed about 95% of the Native American population.

People have all kinds of ideas about how to prevent and treat diseases. Some people think that if you eat lots of onions or garlic, you won't get sick. Others say that you should take huge amounts of vitamins. Scientific
20 experiments have not proved most of these theories. However, people still spend millions of dollars on vitamins and other probably useless treatments or preventatives. Some people want **antibiotics** whenever they get sick. Some antibiotics are very expensive. Much
25 of this money is wasted because some diseases are caused by **viruses.** Viruses are even smaller than bacteria, and they cause different kinds of diseases. Antibiotics are useless against viruses.

People are afraid of many diseases. Because of their
30 fear, people can be **cruel** to victims of disease. Sometimes they **fire** victims from their jobs, throw them out of their apartments, and refuse them transportation **services.** In the epidemics of **plague** a few hundred years ago, people simply covered the doors and windows of the victims'
35 houses and left them inside to die, all in an **effort** to protect themselves from getting sick.

a very serious disease carried by insects

Doctors know how most epidemic diseases spread. Some, like **tuberculosis,** are spread when people **sneeze** and **cough.** The explosive cough or sneeze sends the
40 bacteria shooting out into the air. Then they enter the mouth or nose of anyone nearby.

Others are spread through human contact. When you are sick and blow your nose, you get viruses or bacteria on your hands. Then you touch another
45 person's hand, and when that person touches his or her mouth, nose, or eyes, the disease enters the body. Some diseases spread when people touch the same dishes, towels, and furniture. You can even **pick up** a disease when you touch things in public buildings. Other
50 diseases are spread through insects, such as flies, **mosquitoes,** and **ticks.**

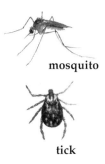

mosquito

tick

248

One disease that causes frequent, worldwide epidemics is **influenza,** or flu for short. The symptoms of influenza include a headache and sometimes a runny nose. Some victims get sick to their stomach. These symptoms are similar to the symptoms of other, milder diseases. About half of all flu patients also have a high body temperature, called a **fever.** Influenza can be a very serious disease, especially for **pregnant** women, people over 65, and people already suffering from another disease such as a heart problem. Flu is very contagious. One person catches the flu from another person; it doesn't begin inside the body as heart disease does.

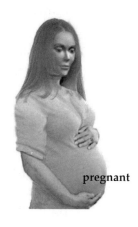
pregnant

Sometimes medicine can relieve the symptoms of a disease. That is, it can make people cough less, make headaches less intense, and stop noses from running for a while. However, medicine can't always cure a disease. So far, there is no cure for many diseases and no medicine to prevent them. People have to try to prevent them in other ways.

Some diseases can be prevented by **vaccination.** A liquid vaccine is **injected** into the arm or taken by mouth, and the person is then safe from catching that disease. Other diseases can be prevented by good health habits, such as drinking only clean water, **boiling** water that might carry disease, and washing the hands often.

Epidemics usually start in areas of large population. Poor people in big cities who live crowded together in **miserable** conditions have the most health problems. They often have the least education about disease prevention. If they know what to do, they often do not have the money to do it. For example, it is difficult for a person who has no electricity to refrigerate food or boil drinking water. With no money, the person can't even buy soap to wash his or her hands.

very bad; inferior

Disease prevention costs much less than disease treatment. It seems completely illogical, but some countries like the United States spend much more health-care money on treatment for diseases than on programs to prevent disease in the first place. Most doctors and other hospital workers stay in their **institutions.** Only a

249

few doctors go out into the streets of the poor areas to educate people. Only a few doctors and some nurses vaccinate people and **supervise** them to make sure they
95 take their medicine. Many people who help poor people with their health problems are volunteers.

How can you use all this information for your own good health? When someone you know becomes ill, try to avoid physical contact with that person. If you get
100 sick yourself, keep your towel and dishes separate from everyone else's. Try not to touch things that belong to others. Don't touch other people, and don't shake hands. Explain why, however; you don't want people to think you are impolite. Wash your hands often if you
105 are ill or if anyone around you is ill.

Researchers continue searching for a way to cure or prevent epidemic diseases. **Meanwhile,** it is worth the money for governments to provide preventive health care for all of their people. Preventing epidemics is
110 much cheaper than stopping them.

a Vocabulary

cough	epidemics	cruel	institutions
meanwhile	picked up	sneeze	miserable
plague	antibiotics	vaccinations	influenza

1. _____ is also called flu.
2. Some diseases are spread when people _____
   and _____ .
3. When you have a headache, you probably feel _____ .
4. Babies should receive _____ to prevent common childhood
   diseases. Then they won't catch these diseases.
5. Governments should provide health care. _____ , they
   should give money for new research into the causes of disease.
6. _____ kill thousands, even millions, of people worldwide.

7. Hospitals and universities are examples of _____.

8. It is very _____ to put a sick person out of his or her house into the street to live.

9. The _____ epidemics killed half the population.

10. If you take _____ too often, they will become ineffective.

11. She thinks she _____ the flu on the long flight to Europe.

b Vocabulary

fever	service	tuberculosis	supervise
fire	effort	viruses	injected
pregnant	boil	mosquitoes	ticks

1. When your temperature is above normal, you have a _____.

2. Your boss can't _____ you without a good reason.

3. Ms. Davis is _____. She is going to have a baby in May.

4. The train _____ in my area is very good. There's a train every fifteen minutes.

5. Diseases caused by _____ cannot be cured with antibiotics.

6. Some vaccines are _____ into the arm; others are taken by mouth.

7. She didn't make any _____ to get a good grade. She didn't study or even come to class. No wonder she failed.

8. If you _____ an egg for ten minutes, it will become hard.

9. There were only two adults to _____ thirty children on the trip.

10. Diseases carried by _____ and _____ enter the victim's blood through the bites of these insects.

11. _____ enters the body when the victim breathes the air coughed out by a sick person.

C Vocabulary Review

raw materials	attacked	dawn	tide
hammer	intensely	apparent	pounded
swell	arteries	forehead	recurring

1. Blood is carried from the heart through the _____.

2. If you hit your thumb with a _____, the thumb will probably _____ up.

3. Sometimes the sky is red at _____.

4. Tom got hit on the _____ with the ball.

5. The army _____ at dawn to surprise the enemy.

6. Rita has a _____ pain in the stomach. It comes and goes.

7. The waves move higher up on the beach as the _____ comes in.

8. Iron and cotton are _____.

9. Dan _____ on the table to get everyone's attention.

10. Everyone in the room was studying the picture _____ when the door opened. No one even noticed that someone came in.

11. It's _____ to me that you didn't read the article. You don't even know what it's about.

d Multiple Choice

1. Coughing is a _____ of tuberculosis.
   a. miserable
   b. epidemic
   c. symptom

2. Medicine can _____ a disease.
   a. cure
   b. relieve the symptoms of
   c. prevent

3. Without the Europeans, North and South America would probably have _____.
   a. more Native Americans
   b. no diseases
   c. no wars

4. Which one of these sentences is *not* true?
   a. Antibiotics can be expensive.
   b. Antibiotics have saved the lives of many sick people.
   c. Antibiotics will help cure diseases caused by viruses.

5. _____ prevent some diseases.
   a. There is no vaccine to
   b. You can have a vaccine injected into your arm to
   c. both a and b

6. Tuberculosis spreads _____ .
   a. by hand contact
   b. when people cough and sneeze
   c. when people don't eat garlic

7. The best way to avoid epidemics is to _____.
   a. lock sick people up inside their houses
   b. take lots of vitamins
   c. provide health care for people in crowded cities

Comprehension Questions

1. Name the symptoms of influenza.
2. What does medicine do for diseases?
3. Is it worth the expense to take extra vitamins?
4. How do epidemics spread?
5. How can epidemics change history?
6. Do you think you should or should not shake hands with someone who is ill? Why?
7. Why do poor people in big cities have the most health problems?
8. Why do people who live in the city have more health problems than people who live in the country (outside of cities)?
9. How can humans prevent diseases from becoming epidemics?

 Main Idea

What is the main idea of each of these paragraphs?

1. Paragraph 2 (lines 10–15)
2. Paragraph 4 (lines 29–36)
3. Paragraph 6 (lines 42–51)
4. Paragraph 9 (lines 71–76)

g Cause and Effect

Write the effect for each of these causes.

Cause	Effect
1. A virus enters the body.	
2. People take medicine.	
3. A person with tuberculosis coughs.	
4. A vaccine is injected into the body.	
5. A student drinks from a sick roommate's glass.	

Word Forms

Choose a word form from the chart for each sentence below. Use the right verb forms and singular or plural nouns.

	Verb	Noun	Adjective	Adverb
1.		(im)politeness	(im)polite	(im)politely
2.		cruelty	cruel	cruelly
3.	relieve	relief	relieved	
4.	volunteer	volunteer	(in)voluntary	(in)voluntarily
5.	inject	injection		
6.		pregnancy	pregnant	
7.		contagion	contagious	contagiously
8.	lengthen	length	long	
9.	reason	reason	(un)reasonable	(un)reasonably

1. The idea of _____ is different from one country to another.
2. It is _____ to hit a very old or sick person.
3. Mary felt _____ when she found out her daughter had arrived safely at her grandparents' home.
4. Mark did not go into the army _____. He went because it is the law that all young men must serve in the army.
5. Children don't like to have _____.
6. A human _____ lasts nine months.
7. Heart trouble is not _____.
8. In the spring, the days start to _____.
9. Mehdi was very angry. We tried to _____ with him, but he was completely _____ and wouldn't listen at all.

i Two-Word Verbs

Learn these two-word verbs and then fill in the blanks with the right words.
Use the correct verb form.

> grow out of = stop doing or feeling (something) as one becomes older
> get out of = avoid doing
> show up   = appear; arrive
> put off   = delay
> read up on = get facts and information on (a subject) by reading

1. Hiroko always tries to _____ talking in front of the class because she doesn't like to do it.
2. Tom had planned to go to the shopping center today, but he _____ it _____ until the weekend because he's so busy.
3. Children _____ sleepwalking when they become adolescents.
4. Marge is going to _____ photovoltaic cells because she wants to know more about them.
5. Bob didn't _____ for the party until almost midnight.

j Articles

Put articles in the blanks if they are needed.

1. Millions of _____ people around _____ world do not have _____ good health care.
2. Sometimes _____ doctor does not know how to treat _____ disease, and sometimes there is no _____ treatment.
3. _____ people have all kinds of _____ ideas about how to prevent and treat _____ diseases.
4. _____ explosive cough or sneeze sends _____ bacteria shooting out into _____ air.
5. Then they enter _____ mouth or nose of _____ anyone nearby.
6. Some diseases spread when _____ people touch _____ same _____ dishes, _____ towels, and _____ furniture.

7. Some countries like _____ United States spend much more health-care money on _____ treatment for diseases than on programs to prevent _____ disease in _____ first place.

 Summarizing

Summarize paragraph 3, lines 16–28. Use your own words to tell the main idea in no more than three or four sentences.

l **Guided Writing**

Write one of these two short compositions.

1. You are a health-care worker who is going into a poor area of a big city. You have seen several cases of tuberculosis and influenza this month. You are going to try to prevent an epidemic among the people in this area. What will you say to the people?
2. A government official in your country has asked you for your suggestions about improving health care. What will you say to the official?

Medicine: From Leeches to Lasers

Before You Read

1. Based on the title of this lesson, what do you think the reading is about?

2. What do you think this doctor is holding up?

3. What are some examples of traditional and modern medicine?

Context Clues

*The words in **bold** print are from this lesson. Use context clues to guess the meaning of each word.*

1. A man named Hippocrates **concluded** that people became sick for natural reasons, not because the gods were angry. He also believed that there was a connection between diet and health.

2. During the time of Hippocrates, doctors **prescribed** massage, special diets, and baths as medical treatments for their patients.

3. In the nineteenth and twentieth centuries, many **remarkable** discoveries were made in medicine. These discoveries saved the lives of millions of people around the world.

4. Hospitals now have large computers and machines that help doctors **diagnose** medical problems.

4 Medicine: From Leeches to Lasers

What do lasers, <u>leeches</u>, tree bark, and old bread have in common? They are all things that people use to make medicine or to help sick people feel better. Throughout history, people have searched for ways to live healthier and better lives. As early as 8000 B.C., people were experimenting with methods of helping sick people. Today, we have very modern technology, yet we continue to look for ways to **improve** medicine and our system of health care.

a type of worm that sucks, or takes in, blood

5

The history of medicine extends back thousands of years. We know that, from the earliest times, people used plants as medicine. Scientists have also found **evidence** that people experimented with <u>surgery</u> 10,000 years ago.

10

People haven't always gone to doctors to get medical help. In Egypt around 3000 B.C., people went to their

opening up the body to fix it

15

priests when they felt sick. That was because many Egyptians believed that the gods made people sick when they were angry with them. Common remedies in Egypt at this time included garlic and

20 onions to prevent epidemics and **moldy** bread to heal wounds. Around this time, however, people in Egypt were also learning more about **sanitation**. Archaeologists there have found the ruins of **elaborate** bathrooms and **sewerage** systems.

having a fungus

ways to keep things clean and germ-free

for the removal of waste

25   In Greece in 410 B.C., a man named Hippocrates **concluded** that people became sick for natural reasons, not because the gods were angry. He also believed that there was a connection between diet and health. During his time, doctors **prescribed** massage, special

30 diets, and baths as medical treatments for their patients.

    In China and other Asian countries, doctors developed acupuncture as a method of treating sickness and pain. Acupuncture uses **needles** to help the human body fight pain and disease. Doctors have used this method for

35 thousands of years, and many still use it today.

    During the Middle Ages (400–1500 A.D.), a few medical schools and hospitals opened in Europe. At this time, however, doctors considered themselves to be primarily observers of patients. For them, surgery was a

40 **menial** task, something a barber should do. One common medical treatment during the Middle Ages was the use of leeches to remove "bad blood" from people. Doctors thought this "bloodletting" was good for many illnesses. Unfortunately, many plagues spread through

low-skill

45 Europe at that time. Doctors could not cure these diseases, and one quarter of the population of Europe died. It didn't help that, in the Middle Ages, many people believed that bathing could be **fatal.** It wasn't uncommon for people to bathe just once a year!

deadly; causing death

50   After the invention of the printing press in the mid-fifteenth century, books on health and medicine became available. Leonardo da Vinci's **drawings** of the human body, including all the muscles, helped doctors tremendously. Understanding the human body helped

55 doctors treat sicknesses and make people feel better.

In the nineteenth and twentieth centuries, many **remarkable** discoveries were made in medicine. These discoveries saved the lives of millions of people around the world. For example, in 1895, a German doctor named
60 Roentgen developed the X-ray machine. In 1928, the English scientist Sir Alexander Fleming discovered penicillin, the first antibiotic. Fleming discovered penicillin growing in mold on an old piece of bread!

Great advances in the technology of medicine
65 continue to be made. Today, doctors can save people's lives by giving them a new heart or a new **kidney**. Hospitals now have large computers and machines that help doctors **diagnose** medical problems.

Although modern medicine is making many new
70 treatments possible, doctors are learning that some of the old ways are useful too. For example, doctors are now paying more attention to the connection between diet and health. Even the leech has found a place in modern medicine. In certain kinds of surgery, up-to-
75 date surgeons are using leeches to prevent a patient's arteries from getting plugged up.

Some people believe that nature has all of the cures for human problems. Others believe that technology is more helpful. It just might be that, together, tradition
80 and technology will help people everywhere live better and healthier lives.

a Vocabulary

improve	evidence	surgery	sanitation
leech	elaborate	sewerage	concluded
needle	menial	fatal	drawing

1. They have an _____ garden behind their house. They must work on it for hours every day.

2. After carefully studying the X-ray of his arm, the doctors _____ that it wasn't broken.

3. The doctors gave the patient something to make him sleep during _____ .

4. The _____ Department in our city has to inspect all restaurants to make sure that they are clean.

5. During the bad storm, all the _____ from the city went right into the river.

6. A doctor uses a _____ when she gives you an injection.

7. When he walked out of the lake, there was a _____ on his leg.

8. I don't mind doing _____ jobs, because I can think about other things at the same time.

9. He said that his neighbor stole his boat, but he didn't have any _____ to prove it.

10. You will probably feel better if you _____ your diet.

b Vocabulary

moldy	kidneys	diagnose	fatal
draw	unsanitary	evident	improvement
conclusion	needle	surgeon	

1. If you leave the bread out for too long, it will get _____.
2. The doctors needed several X-rays before they could _____ his problem.
3. Luckily everyone in the car was wearing a seatbelt. Otherwise, it might have been a _____ accident.
4. I can't understand your directions. Could you _____ me a map?
5. Most people have two _____ located in their lower back.
6. It's _____ to handle food without first washing your hands.
7. At the _____ of the movie, everyone died.
8. The patient made great _____ in the week after surgery.

c Vocabulary Review: Synonyms

Match the words that mean the same.

_____ 1. analyze	a. a lot
_____ 2. miserable	b. blur
_____ 3. blank	c. teenager
_____ 4. a great deal	d. study
_____ 5. meanwhile	e. vision
_____ 6. nightmare	f. forever
_____ 7. confused	g. at the same time
_____ 8. adolescent	h. location
_____ 9. permanently	i. painful
_____ 10. sore	j. unhappy
_____ 11. dawn	k. empty
_____ 12. position	l. sunrise
	m. mixed up
	n. bad dream

Lesson 4: Medicine: From Leeches to Lasers

d True/False/No Information

_____ 1. Surgery is a very recent type of medical treatment.
_____ 2. Doctors were very busy in ancient Egypt.
_____ 3. People weren't interested in cleanliness until the
           nineteenth century.
_____ 4. Leeches have always been used to help patients.
_____ 5. Acupuncture was not popular in Europe during the Middle Ages.
_____ 6. Leonardo da Vinci was a medical doctor.
_____ 7. The X-ray machine was developed before the discovery
           of penicillin.
_____ 8. An X-ray machine can help doctors diagnose a broken bone.
_____ 9. There is no good reason for doctors to study cures and treatments
           of the past.
_____ 10. The first antibiotic was found growing on bread.

e Comprehension Questions

1. When did doctors first do surgery?
2. Why did Egyptians go to their priests for medical help instead of to
   their doctors?
3. What was medical care like in ancient Egypt?
4. Compare the medical care in Egypt in 3000 B.C. and in Greece in 410 B.C.
5. What is acupuncture?
6. What was unusual about a doctor's work in the Middle Ages in Europe?
7. What effect did the invention of the printing press have on medical care?
8. What do you think is one of the most remarkable discoveries in
   medicine? Why?

f Main Idea

What is the main idea of each of these paragraphs?

1. Paragraph 2 (lines 10–13)
2. Paragraph 5 (lines 31–35)
3. Paragraph 7 (lines 50–55)

g Prepositions

Put the right preposition in each blank.

1. What do lasers, leeches, tree bark, and old bread have _____ common?

2. Throughout history, people have searched _____ ways to live healthier and better lives.

3. In China and other Asian countries, doctors developed acupuncture _____ a method _____ treating sickness and pain.

4. Doctors have used this method _____ thousands of years.

5. After the invention _____ the printing press _____ the mid-fifteenth century, books _____ health and medicine became available.

6. Great advances _____ the technology _____ medicine continue to be made.

7. Today, doctors can save people's lives _____ giving them a new heart.

h Compound Words and Two-Word Verbs

Make a compound word by joining a word from the first column with one from the second column. More than one answer is correct for several of the words. Some of these compounds are also written separately as two-word verbs.

_____	1. break	a. in
_____	2. stand	b. down
_____	3. work	c. work
_____	4. check	d. mate
_____	5. sun	e. rise
_____	6. home	f. night
_____	7. sleep	g. by
_____	8. out	h. grow
_____	9. life	i. walk
_____	10. over	j. way
_____	11. air	k. time
_____	12. room	l. out

i Word Forms

Choose a word form from the chart for each sentence below. Use the right verb forms and singular or plural nouns.

	Verb	Noun	Adjective	Adverb
1.	improve	improvement		
2.		evidence	evident	evidently
3.		sanitation	(un)sanitary	(un)sanitarily
4.	elaborate	elaboration	elaborate	elaborately
5.		similarity	(dis)similar	(dis)similarly
6.	prescribe	prescription		
7.	medicate	medicine	medical	medically
8.		fatality	fatal	fatally
9.	diagnose	diagnosis	diagnostic	diagnostically

1. There has been a tremendous _____ in surgical methods over the past century.
2. The newspaper gave a great description of the event. _____, someone from the newspaper saw the whole thing.
3. Everything in the operating room must be _____.
4. I don't understand your explanation. Could you please _____?
5. What is the _____ between snow and hail?
6. What did the doctor _____ for your headache? Did he give you a _____?
7. Jane wants to go to _____ college and become a doctor.
8. There were two _____ in yesterday's car accident on Route 34.
9. She went to three different doctors to get a _____.

Summarizing

Write a summary of the text for this lesson. Write only the most important information, using three to five sentences.

 Guided Writing

Write one of these two short compositions.

1. What would you like and not like about being a doctor during the Middle Ages in Europe?
2. Do you think it's important to study the history of medicine? Why or why not?

lesson
5

Cholesterol and
Heart Disease

© Paul Barton/CORBIS

Before You Read

1. Do you have a healthy diet? Why do you think so?

2. What effect can exercise have on heart disease?

3. Is it difficult or easy to change your lifestyle? Why?

Context Clues

*The words in **bold** print are from this lesson. Use context clues to guess the meaning of each word.*

1. Some people say that heart disease is not really a serious problem. They think the danger of heart disease is **exaggerated.**

2. A natural substance in the blood, **cholesterol** comes from the liver.

3. **Angiograms** are X-rays of the heart arteries.

4. People often **complain** about low-fat diets. They say that the food doesn't taste good.

5. Doctors can use a special camera to watch a person's blood **circulating** through the arteries.

5   Cholesterol and Heart Disease

Do you know your **cholesterol** level? A high level of cholesterol in the blood is an important **risk factor** for heart disease, so it's a good idea to know your cholesterol level.

5   Some people say that the danger of heart disease is <u>**exaggerated.**</u> However, heart disease is a main cause of death in developed countries. Every year, more than 1 million Americans have heart attacks, and half of them die. People with heart disease suffer chest pains

10   that make simple activities, such as walking, shaving, or taking a shower, difficult.

Research has proven that cholesterol levels are connected with heart disease. One project in Massachusetts has studied the same group of fifteen

15   men and women since 1948. The researchers have found

said to be more than it is

269

that the people who have high levels of cholesterol have more heart attacks.

A natural **substance** in the blood, cholesterol comes from the liver. The amount of cholesterol is affected
20 by diet and by physical qualities people <u>inherit</u> from their parents. One kind of cholesterol sticks fat to the walls of arteries, making the arteries smaller and finally blocking them. It produces a condition called "hardening of the arteries," which causes heart attacks.
25 With tiny cameras, doctors can see blood **circulating** through the heart <u>valves</u>. **Angiograms** are X-rays of the heart arteries. They show fat **deposits** and blockages caused by high cholesterol.

get

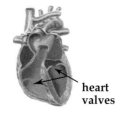

heart valves

Heart disease begins in children as young as 3 years
30 old. It occurs earlier in boys than in girls. Nearly half of teenagers have some fat deposits on their artery walls. Heart disease develops faster if you have a high cholesterol level and you also smoke.

What is a safe level of cholesterol? Adults have a
35 high risk of heart attack if their cholesterol level is above 240 milligrams per deciliter of blood. Below 200 is better. In the Massachusetts study, no one with a cholesterol level below 150 has ever had a heart attack. However, about half of American adults have
40 cholesterol levels above 200.

To lower your cholesterol level, you must change your eating habits. Anything that comes from an animal is high in fat and high in cholesterol. The American Heart Association National Cholesterol Education
45 Program says that fat should be no more than 30% of your diet. Blood cholesterol levels start to fall after two to three weeks of following a low-cholesterol, low-fat diet. Dietary changes alone can result in a 10% <u>reduction</u> of the average person's cholesterol level.

decrease

50 <u>Aerobic</u> exercise helps, too. Artery blockage can be reduced by as much as 40% through changes in diet and amount of exercise.

increasing oxygen intake (for example, walking, running, and swimming are aerobic exercise)

We should educate everyone, including children in elementary schools, about the danger of cholesterol. We
55 should teach them responsibility for their health

through classes in nutrition and aerobic exercise. For example, the smart **snack** is fruit. Children should be served fruit in the school cafeteria, along with low-fat meals. Schools should send **recipes** home with children.

60 Parents should include children in planning and preparing meals and shopping for food.

Adults, including people over the age of 65, can lower their cholesterol by 30 or 40%. It is never too late to change. One man began his health program when he

65 was 73. By the time he was 77, he had lowered his arterial blockage from 50% to 13% and his cholesterol from 320 to 145 without drugs. He went on a vegetarian diet with only 10% fat and followed programs to reduce stress and get more exercise.

70 A low-cholesterol diet that cuts out most animal products and high-fat vegetables may be **unfamiliar** to people. The Heart Association says to use no added fat of any kind. Don't fry food in oil. Cook it in water, vinegar, or vegetable water. Learn about grains and

75 vegetables. Avoid egg yolks (the yellow part of the egg). Eat potatoes, beans, low-fat vegetables, and fruit. People often **complain** about low-fat diets before they have had time to get used to them. Food can taste good without cream, butter, and salt. You can use olive oil, mustard,

80 fresh **herbs,** or yogurt instead.

A new diet can cause general **anxiety,** when people feel worried and nervous about what is going to happen. They must learn to **deal with** the changes in their lives. Sometimes major changes in diet or lifestyle

85 are easier than minor ones because the results are bigger and occur faster. Fast results **encourage** us.

How can you control the amount of fat in your diet if you eat in restaurants? Restaurants should provide healthy meals that are low in fat, salt, and cholesterol. A

90 diet is a **personal** thing. Restaurant owners should not make customers feel embarrassed because they want to follow a diet that is good for them. Restaurant owners must learn to give equal service to customers on a healthy diet. Some restaurants have items on the menu

95 marked with a heart to show that they are low in fat,

something small that can be eaten fast

instructions for cooking

strange; unknown

say they don't like

cope with

private; about oneself

271

cholesterol, salt, and/or sugar. A few restaurants serve only these items.

Education programs, such as the American Heart Association National Cholesterol Education Program,
100 cost money but can bring results. In 1983, only 35% of the American public knew their cholesterol levels. By 2000, 60% of the people had had theirs checked.

People feel better if they lower their cholesterol through diet. Healthy people are more **confident.** They
105 are more <u>attractive</u> to themselves, as well as to others.   pretty; handsome
Their friends <u>stare</u> at them because they look so healthy.   look intensely

We can prevent heart disease by living a healthful lifestyle and eating the right kind of diet. If people don't do this, two out of three men and women in the
110 United States will eventually get heart disease.

a   Vocabulary

confidence	anxiety	stare	herbs
aerobic	risk	encouraged	valve
unfamiliar	inherited	personal	snack

1. John's parents _____ him to stay in school, even though his grades were not very good.

2. _____ exercise is good for the heart.

3. Is it impolite to ask someone _____ questions?

4. Students often suffer from _____ before an exam.

5. _____ improve the taste of food.

6. Some people are _____ with a low-fat diet.

7. Mark _____ red hair from his mother.

8. It is impolite to _____ at people.

9. If you drive carelessly, you take a _____.

10. I'm hungry now, but it's two hours until dinner. I think I'll have a _____.

11. Open the _____ so that the water will flow freely through the pipes.

12. If you are sure of yourself, you have _____ in yourself.

b Vocabulary

factor	circulated	deal with	complains
attractive	reduction	deposit	angiogram
exaggerated	cholesterol	recipe	substance

1. Many television stars are _____.

2. _____ occurs naturally in the blood.

3. A _____ in how much fat you eat might make you healthier.

4. Please give me a copy of the _____ for that delicious soup.

5. Please _____ your books in the box at the back of the room.

6. It is difficult to _____ a child who doesn't behave well.

7. Smoking is a _____ in many diseases of the heart and lungs.

8. Tom said that he earned $1,000 a week, but he is really paid only $800. He _____.

9. The doctor wants my mother to have an _____ to see if her arteries are blocked.

10. Ali always _____ that he has too much homework.

11. There's a strange _____ on the table. It looks like water, but it isn't.

12. While the students were reading, the teacher _____ around the room to ask them questions.

c Vocabulary Review: Definitions

Match the words with the definitions.

_____ 1. tremendously	a. length of time	
_____ 2. period	b. at the same time	
_____ 3. habit	c. stage	
_____ 4. meanwhile	d. germ free	
_____ 5. fever	e. grind	
_____ 6. pregnant	f. something that supports a statement	
_____ 7. elaborate	g. watch	
_____ 8. evidence	h. very detailed	
_____ 9. sanitary	i. anxious	
_____ 10. solar	j. usual action	
_____ 11. observe	k. high body temperature	
	l. of the sun	
	m. very much	
	n. going to become a mother	

d True/False/Not Enough Information

_____ 1. About 500,000 Americans die each year from heart disease.

_____ 2. More than twice as many people had their blood cholesterol levels checked in 2000 as in 1983.

_____ 3. Smoking can be a risk factor for heart disease.

_____ 4. No direct relationship has been proven between high cholesterol levels and heart attacks.

_____ 5. Girls have no risk of heart disease.

_____ 6. Low-fat diets always taste bad.

_____ 7. Children should learn more responsibility for eating healthful food.

_____ 8. People usually feel good about going on a new diet.

_____ 9. It can be easier to change our diet a lot than to change it a little.

_____ 10. Old people shouldn't bother to change their eating habits because it's too late for it to do them any good.

e Comprehension Questions

1. What are some symptoms of heart disease?
2. What is hardening of the arteries? How is it connected with high cholesterol?
3. Why are angiograms useful?
4. At what age does heart disease start?
5. What level of cholesterol is believed to be safe?
6. How long does it take for cholesterol levels to start to drop?
7. How can parents help teach children healthy eating habits?
8. What are some ways to reduce fat in your diet?

f Main Idea

What is the main idea of each of these paragraphs?

1. Paragraph 4 (lines 18–28)
2. Paragraph 6 (lines 34–40)
3. Paragraph 9 (lines 62–69)

g Word Forms

Choose a word form from the chart for each sentence below. Use the right verb forms and singular or plural nouns.

	Verb	Noun	Adjective	Adverb
1.		anxiety	anxious	anxiously
2.	encourage	encouragement	encouraged	encouragingly
3.	discourage	discouragement	discouraged	discouragingly
4.		stress	stressful	stressfully
5.	personalize	person	personal	personally
6.		stupidity	stupid	stupidly
7.	attract	attraction	(un)attractive	(un)attractively
8.	inherit	inheritance	inherited	
9.	familiarize	familiarity	(un)familiar	familiarly
10.	suggest	suggestion	suggested	
11.	complain	complaint		complainingly
12.	exaggerate	exaggeration	exaggerated	exaggeratedly
13.	serve	service		

1. The students waited _____ to hear the results of the test.
2. Marie was _____ by the results of her physical exam after a long illness.
3. Michael felt _____ when he wasn't accepted at the university that was his first choice.
4. Joan felt a lot of _____ when she stood before the class and began her speech.
5. _____, I don't mind if people use their cell phones on the train.
6. Marie felt _____ because she did the exercise without reading the directions and did it all wrong.

7. Honey _____ flies. Ants also are _____ by honey.

8. Tom _____ a small business and some money from his father when his father died. His friend received a large _____ from his favorite uncle.

9. If you _____ yourself with the language center before the first day of classes, you will not get confused about where you should go.

10. I _____ that we take an exercise class this month. That's a good _____.

11. If you have any _____ about the television set you bought, take it back to the store.

12. To say that you couldn't get to sleep at all last night is an _____. You are _____.

13. A waiter _____ food in a restaurant.

h Irregular Verbs

Learn these verbs. Then put the right verb forms in the blanks in the sentences below. Use the first verb in the first sentence, and so on.

Simple	Past	Past Participle
1. tear	tore	torn
2. light	lit or lighted	lit or lighted
3. lie	lay	lain
4. swell	swelled	swollen
5. grind	ground	ground
6. draw	drew	drawn
7. stick	stuck	stuck
8. deal	dealt	dealt

1. Alice _____ her new blouse.

2. Dan _____ a fire in the living room fireplace.

3. In some countries, it is the custom to _____ down for a rest in the middle of the day.

4. Ms. Baxter's hand is _____ because she shut it in the car door.

5. Mr. Thomas _____ some fresh coffee beans and made coffee.

6. The children _____ a picture of a big animal on the wall outside their school.

7. The roadrunner _____ out its head when it runs.

8. Mr. Nevins is a car dealer. He _____ in new and used cars.

i Two-Word Verbs: Review

1. Sixteen people showed _____ for volleyball practice.

2. Never put _____ until tomorrow what you can do today.

3. What time does your plane get _____?

4. Were you brought _____ in the city or in the country?

5. When he wrote the class list, the teacher left _____ one student.

6. Do you dress _____ for dinner at an expensive restaurant?

7. Look _____! There's a hole in the sidewalk.

8. I have to read _____ _____ a subject for my speech.

9. Kim had _____ a warm jacket so I knew it was cold outside.

10. The Bakers have to buy new shoes for their daughter. She grew _____ _____ her old ones.

11. We tried to get _____ _____ helping our cousin, but we had to do it.

j Context Clues

*Each of the words in **bold** has more than one meaning. Circle the letter of the best meaning of the word as it is used in the sentence.*

1. Mr. Becker has worked in the **field** of computer science for ten years.
   a. area of specialization
   b. place where animals or plants are raised
   c. place where baseball is played

2. Carolyn is often late for class because she has to walk **so far** from her apartment.
   a. until now
   b. such a long distance
   c. far enough

3. There are 2.2 **pounds** in a kilo.
   a. unit of English money
   b. hits or strikes
   c. unit of weight

4. Trappers sometimes **cure** the skins of the animals they catch before they sell the skins.
   a. dry and prepare for use
   b. make better
   c. a kind of medicine

5. The **current** value of gold is $321 an ounce.
   a. movement of electricity
   b. at this time
   c. movement of a stream of water in the ocean

6. I know that it isn't **so**.
   a. very
   b. therefore
   c. true

7. Ali and Muhammed live in a large apartment **complex** near the university.
   a. related group of buildings
   b. complicated
   c. anxiety

 Summarizing

Write a summary of the text for this lesson. Write only the important information, using three to five sentences.

Guided Writing

Write one of these two short compositions.

1. You are going to start an educational program about heart disease in your area. How will you do this?
2. Your doctor told you that you have to lower your cholesterol. Give a detailed plan of how you will follow the doctor's suggestion.

Video Highlights

a Before You Watch

1. Discuss the questions below with your classmates.
   a. Do you enjoy going to the doctor? Why or why not?
   b. The word *cardio-* is a medical word for *heart*. What kind of doctor is a cardiologist?
   c. Have you seen the picture on the right before? What does it mean?

2. The video you are going to watch is about a man who has two jobs. Dr. Cleve Francis is a doctor and a country music performer. Discuss the advantages and disadvantages of both jobs. Then complete the chart below. List as many advantages and disadvantages as you can.

	Advantages	Disadvantages
Doctor	1. *good salary* 2. 3.	1. *long hours* 2. 3.
Country music performer	1. 2. 3.	1. 2. 3.

b   As You Watch

Complete these sentences about Dr. Francis's two careers.

1. Dr. Francis has spent his medical career treating patients
   with _____.
2. Now he's singing about the pains of a _____.

c   After You Watch

1. Watch the video again. Then read the following excerpts.
   What conclusion can you draw about Cleve Francis from each
   one? Check your choices.
   a. "Things are looking bright for Cleve Francis. The 46-year-
      old heart doctor is undergoing a transformation to country
      music performer."
      ☐ He is happy about the change.
      ☐ He is sorry to leave his career as a cardiologist.
      ☐ He believes that he is too old to make a career change.
   b. "Francis's journey into country has another trail-blazing
      aspect. There are few Black performers in the field."
      ☐ Dr. Francis is not unusual.
      ☐ There are not many African-American cardiologists.
      ☐ Most country music performers are not black.

2. In the video, Dr. Francis expresses several opinions. Do you
   agree or disagree or have no opinion? Explain your responses
   to a small group of your classmates.
   a. "There is a link between music and medicine."
      ☐ agree   ☐ disagree   ☐ no opinion
   b. "If you took away the music, books, and paintings . . . life
      would
      be bare."
      ☐ agree   ☐ disagree   ☐ no opinion
   c. "The older you are, the better."
      ☐ agree   ☐ disagree   ☐ no opinion

Who Said What?

Play this game with a group of your classmates. Choose one student in the group to be the Game Host and another to be the Judge. The rest of the students will be on Team A or Team B. All students except the Host and the Judge must keep their books closed during the game.

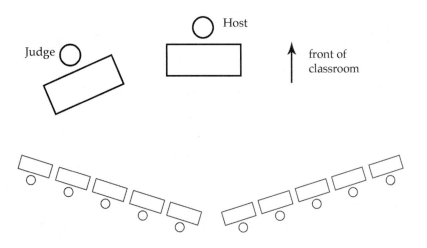

Host: Follow these three steps to begin the game.

1. Write this list on the board:

Robert Louis Stevenson	English writer
Cleve Francis	American cardiologist and singer
Louis Armstrong	American jazz trumpeter
Benjamin Franklin	American philosopher
John F. Kennedy	American president
Madonna	American singer
Robert Hunter	American environmentalist

2. Read this introduction aloud to the two teams:

   "I am going to read a quotation aloud. One person on a team will have a chance to guess which of these people said it. If that person gets it wrong, a person on the other team gets a chance. Are you ready?"

3. Choose a quotation from this list. Ask Team A first, then Team B, and so on.

   a. "All music is folk music. I haven't ever heard a horse sing a song."
   b. "Ask not what your country can do for you, ask what you can do for your country."
   c. "We are living in a material world, and I am a material girl."
   d. "Early to bed and early to rise makes a man healthy, wealthy, and wise."
   e. "Our responsibility is to protect the Earth for a million years."
   f. "I'm not leading a Civil Rights march into country music."

Judge: Check the team's answer and declare it "right" or "wrong": (a) Louis Armstrong (b) John F. Kennedy (c) Madonna (d) Benjamin Franklin (e) Robert Hunter (f) Cleve Francis

Learning About Word Stress

Your dictionary shows which syllable in a word is stressed. The mark showing the syllable with primary (heaviest) stress in the word *influenza* is pointed out below.

primary stress

in-flu-en-za /ˌɪnfluˈɛnzə/ *n.* [U] a contagious illness spread by viruses: *Influenza killed millions in 1918, but now there is a shot that prevents it.*

1. Look up these words and underline the syllable with primary stress. Practice saying the words with a partner.

   Example: influ<u>en</u>za

antibiotic	malaria
anxiety	medicine
caffeine	mosquito
cancer	nightmare
diet	resuscitation
exercise	surgery
bacteria	tuberculosis
headache	vaccination

2. Now group the words in the chart below.

Health Problems	**Causes**	**Solutions**
malaria	*mosquito*	*medicine*

Vocabulary

a

a great deal   237
aborigines   3
accident   124
active   213
actually   100
addictive   239
adjust   155
adolescents   238
adopted   13
advancements   145
advantages   145
aerobic   270
afford   70
agricultural   80
alarm   211
already   58
alternating   191
analyze   228
angiograms   270
anthropologists   155
antibiotics   248
anxiety   271
apparent   239
archaeologists   99
architects   145
arteries   227
articles   12
as well as   80
ashore   23
aspirin   228
astonishing   190
at times   32
atmosphere   190
attacks   212
attractive   272
available   58

b

backwards   155
bacteria   170
balance   169
base   3
batteries   100
beams   145
beggar   13
belongings   32
bilingual   135
biological   210
blank   238
blind   32
blizzards   31
block   239
blurred   227
bodies   32
boiling   249
bombs   146
borders   12
borrow   134
bothers   124
boundary   200
brain   135
branches   89
broad   154
broke down   31
built   3
burst   180

c

caffeine   212
carbon dioxide   170
carpet   90
carries   114
cave   12
centers   146
characters   133
childhood   12
cholesterol   269
chosen   3
chronic   58
circulating   270
civil war   13
clear   90
clockwise   156
cluster   228
colonies   169
combined   58
commercial   59
complain   271
complex   169
concentrate   238
concluded   260
conductor   200
confident   272
confused   238
consider   169
consists of   69
converted   200
cope   180
cough   248
counterclockwise   156
crash   123
creating   170
creatures   41
crucial   58
cruel   248
crush   42
crushed   180
cylinder   42

d

dawn   211
deal with   271
debris   180
decades   23
deep (serious)   101
delays   22
demand   58
density   42
depends on   58
deposits   270
descend   42
designing   145
destruction   90
details   12
developed   59
diagnose   261
diameter   42
diet   114
dispose of   100
diversity   43
divided   134
divorce   71
domestic   80
drawings   260

e

earthquakes   146
edge   31
education   156
effect   59
efficiently   200
effort   248
elaborate   260
elements   169
emphasis   70
empty   91
enclosed   42
encourage   271
end up   100
endangering   32
epicenter   178
epidemics   247

287

erupted   180
escaped   12
especially   79
estimate   135
even though   115
evidence   259
exactly   146
exaggerated   269
exhausted   32
exist   199
expedition   3
experts   43
exploration   4
export   201
extended   69
extremely   31

fast   212
fatal   260
fear   123
feast   212
fever   249
fields   80
finally   3
financially   70
fingerprint   190
fire (v.)   248
fits (into)   115
floating   180
flood   178
forced   154
forehead   228
forming   133
fresh   23
fuel   32

garbage   99
gathered   23
geography   22
geothermal   181
get along   4
gradually   57
grow up   69

habit   238
halfway   3
hammer   227
hampered   42
harmless   123
hazardous   100
headache   227
heartbeat   211
heights   123
helmet   42
hemisphere   3
herbs   271
heroes   4
hollow   42
household   70
humidity   89

illiterate   80
immigrants   145
import   201
improve   259
in addition   145
in general   125
in good company
   156
in order to   22
incentive   42
included   22
industrialization   70
inexhaustible   199
influenza   249
inherit   270
injected   249
inland   31
institutions   249
instructors   125
intense   238
interior   3
investigating   99

jaw   238
jet lag   210

joined   22
journalist   12

keep from   171
kidney   261
knocks   114

laboratory   169
lack   23
landfills   99
last   59
layer   178
leaves   90
leeches   259
lessen   212
level   89
lifestyle   228
lifts   115
lightning   180
like   13
likely   155
limited   58
linguists   135
lives on   33
logical   123
loneliness   4
loose   212
loss   124

magic   199
majority   70
married couple   69
mate   114
mathematicians   191
matter   91
maybe   115
meaningful   133
meanwhile   250
melted   180
memorize   154
menial   260
microscopic   190

mid-   191
migraine   227
migrate   211
mild   178
miserable   249
mistake   32
modern   99
moisture   89
moldy   260
mosquitoes   248
multiple   191

n

natural resources   58
nearly   80
necessary   154
needles   260
negative   80
nest   114
network   41
nightmares   238
no longer   91
nonrenewable   59
nuclear   69
nutrients   90

o

observes   181
occurs   190
of course   80
official   79
on the other hand
   100
once in a while   114
opportunities   70
opposite   156
orders   3
ordinarily   191
organization   30
oxygen   91

p

pain   227
passed (a law)   79
past   135

288

paths 90
patient 228
pattern 191
periods 238
permanent 239
permitting 156
personal 271
phobia 123
photovoltaic cell
  199
physical 228
physicist 170
pick up (catch) 248
plague 248
planets 169
pleasant 145
positions 80
positive 79
pounding 227
predict 57
prefer 154
pregnant 249
prescribed 260
presents 114
pressure 42
projects 169
property 180
proved 23
provide for 32
psychologists 125
public 145
published 79

ran away 12
ranged 179
rate 135
rather 41
raw materials 201
real 12
realized 23
reasonable 200
rechargeable 100
recipes 271
recurring 228
recyclables 100
reduction 270
referred to 134

region 89
relatives 70
relief 238
reluctant 201
remained 13
remaining 90
remarkable 261
remind 23
remote 13
research 13
respond 154
revealed 100
rhythm 210
risk factor 269
rolling 178
roots 90
roughly 41

sanitation 260
satellites 170
scattered 179
science fiction 169
search party 4
secret 12
seismic 178
seismology 181
semiconductors
  200
senses 154
separate 23
services 248
sewerage 260
shy 114
signal 211
silicon 200
simple 191
since 200
situation 124
skilled 22
skyscraper 144
snack 271
snakes 114
sneeze 248
snoring 239
snowflake 190
so 191
so far 170

sociologists 71
solar 170
soldiers 22
solid-state 200
sore 228
sources 59
space 146
specialists 134
species 42
spiders 114
spot 115
stabilized 71
stages 237
standard of living
  58
stare 272
steady 228
stealing 144
sticks out 114
story 145
straight 113
stuttering 155
substance 270
such as 90
suffer 155
supervise 250
supplies 3
supported 12
surface 41
surgery 259
surprising 90
surrounded 12
swamps 3
sweating 238
swell 227
system 133

take care of 70
takeoff 125
tasks 70
technologies 58
temperate 210
temperatures 13
tension 228
terrifying 123
threatened 58
through 90

throughout 79
thunder 180
ticks 248
tides 211
title 144
tons 22
tools 155
traffic 124
transparent 200
trapped 190
tremendously 70
tuberculosis 248
tunnel 124
turn into 3

uneven 31
unfamiliar 271
unique 180
unsuccessful 91
up to 191

v

vaccination 249
valves 270
vibrations 178
victims 180
viruses 248
vision 227
vitamin 23
volcano 180
vomit 227

w

warning 227
waste 100
weak 31
whistles 114
wide awake 210
workforce 80

z

zone 113

289

Skills Index

ACTIVITY PAGE
Adventure trail, 52
Crossword puzzles, 109, 222
Phrases, 165
Who said what?, 283–284

CHARTS
Antonyms, 183
Cause and effect, 174, 254
Dictionary research, 224
Reading, 83–84
Scanning, 233
Synonyms, 183
Word forms, 17, 37, 47, 66, 75, 86, 95, 118–119,
129, 140, 150, 159, 185, 207, 232, 244, 255,
266, 276
Word stress, 285
Writing, 162, 281
Writing notes, 108

DICTIONARY PAGE
Definitions, 53–54
Dictionary research, 223–224
Grammar codes, 166
Word forms, 110
Word stress, 285

MAPS
Reading, 220

PUNCTUATION
Adverbs, 129

READING
Cause and effect, 95, 174, 254
Charts, 83–84
Comprehension, 7, 16, 26, 36, 38, 46, 63–64, 74,
84, 94, 104, 118, 128, 138, 149, 159, 162, 174,
184, 194, 204, 215, 231–232, 242, 254, 264,
275
Main ideas, 8, 16, 26, 36, 46, 64, 74, 84, 94, 104,
106, 118, 128, 138, 149, 159, 174, 184, 194,
204, 216, 232, 242, 254, 264, 275
Maps, 220
Paraphrasing, 94, 138, 184
Prereading activities, 2, 10, 20, 29, 40, 56, 68, 78,
88, 98, 112, 122, 132, 143, 153, 168, 177, 189,
198, 209, 226, 236, 246, 258, 268
Rereading, 27
Scanning, 46, 85, 139, 186, 204, 233, 242

Sentences, 110
Speed, 26–27
Vocabulary, 5–6, 14–15, 24–25, 33–34, 44–45,
60–61, 72–73, 81–82, 92–93, 102–103,
115–117, 125–126, 135–137, 146–148,
156–158, 171–173, 181–183, 192–193,
202–203, 213–215, 229–230, 250–252,
262–263, 272–274
  Antonyms, 34, 103, 137, 183, 230
  Context clues, 11, 21, 30, 41, 57, 69, 79, 89, 99,
  113, 123, 133, 144, 154, 169, 178, 190, 199,
  210, 227, 237, 247, 259, 269, 278–279
  Synonyms, 93, 183

SPEAKING
Discussion, 51, 163, 164, 220, 281, 282
Partner activities, 221, 285

TEST-TAKING SKILLS
Choosing item that does not belong, 126, 203
Comprehension questions, 7, 16, 26, 36, 46,
63–64, 74, 84, 94, 104, 118, 128, 138, 149,
159, 174, 184, 194, 204, 215, 231–232, 242,
254, 264, 275
Fill in blanks, 5–6, 8, 9, 14–15, 17–18, 19, 24–25,
27–28, 33–34, 37, 38, 39, 44–45, 47–48, 49,
54, 60–61, 64, 65, 66, 67, 72–73, 75–76,
81–82, 85, 86, 92–93, 95–97, 102–103, 105,
115–116, 119, 120, 125–126, 129, 130,
135–136, 140, 141, 142, 146–147, 150–151,
156–158, 160–161, 171–173, 175–176,
181–182, 185–187, 192–193, 195–196,
202–203, 205–206, 207, 213–215, 216,
217–218, 220, 221, 229–230, 233, 234,
240–241, 243, 244–245, 250–252, 255,
256–257, 262–263, 265, 266, 272–273,
276–279
Matching, 25, 34, 51, 53, 73, 82, 93, 95, 103, 116,
137, 148, 193, 230, 241, 263, 274
Multiple-choice questions, 8, 15, 16, 26, 35, 36,
46, 62–63, 83–84, 103–104, 121, 127,
148–149, 173, 203–204, 221, 230–231, 253,
278–279, 282
Sentence completion, 51, 110, 166, 282
Sequencing, 187, 218
Short-answer questions, 46, 85, 187, 194, 242
True/false/not enough information questions,
25, 45, 73–74, 93–94, 117, 137, 158, 183–184,
215, 241–242, 264, 274

291

True/false questions, 7, 107

TOPICS
Explorers, 1–54
  Bering: Bering Strait, 20–28
  Burke and Wills: Australia, 2–9
  David-Neel: Tibet, 10–19
  Ocean exploration, 40–49
  Scott: South Pole, 29–39
Fear of flying, 122–131
Languages and language diversity, 132–142
Left-handedness, 153–162
Medicine and health, 225–285
  Advances in medicine, 258–267
  Cholesterol and heart disease, 268–280
  Headaches, 226–235
  Health care and epidemics, 246–257
  Sleep and dreams, 236–245
Roadrunners, 112–121
Science, 167–224
  Biological clocks, 209–219
  Biospheres in space, 168–176
  Earthquakes, 177–188
  Photovoltaic cells, 198–208
  Snow and hail, 189–197
Skyscrapers, 143–152
World issues, 55–108
  Families, 68–77
  Garbage Project, 98–106
  Population growth, 56–67
  Rain forests, 88–97
  Women, 78–87

VIEWING
Partner activities, 50, 107, 163
Video highlights, 50–51, 107–108, 163–164,
    220–221, 281–282

WORD STUDY
Active and passive sentences, 139
Adjectives, 17–18, 37, 47, 65, 66, 75, 86, 95–96,
    108, 110, 119, 129, 140, 159–160, 185–186,
    207, 232– 233, 244–245, 255, 266, 276
  Adjectives following verbs, 235
  -ed form, 216
  -ing form, 216
  Participles, 65
  Sentence forms, 206
  Suffixes, 75
Adverbs, 17–18, 37, 47, 66, 86, 95–96, 119, 140,
    159–160, 185–186, 207, 232–233, 244–245,
    255, 266, 276
  -ly ending, 128
  Punctuation, 129
Articles, 9, 18, 48–49, 67, 76, 85–86, 96–97, 130,
    141, 151, 175–176, 195–196, 234, 256–257

Collocations, 39
Compound words, 19, 105, 196, 265
Connecting words
  after, 161, 243
  although, 243
  and, 106, 130
  before, 161, 243
  but, 87, 130
  even though, 120, 130, 218
  since, 161, 218, 243
  until, 161, 218
  when, 161
Nouns, 17–18, 36–37, 47, 66, 86, 95–96, 110, 118,
    119, 129, 140, 159–160, 175, 185–186, 207,
    232–233, 244–245, 255, 266, 276
  Noun substitutes, 96, 141, 175, 234
  Suffixes, 47
Prefixes
  Negative prefixes, 195
  semi-, 217
  Verbs, 150
Prepositions, 28, 48, 120, 217–218, 265
Sentence parts, 36
Suffixes
  Adjectives, 75
  Nouns, 47
  Verbs, 150
Verbs, 17–18, 27, 37, 47, 66, 86, 95–96, 110, 119,
    129, 140, 159–160, 175, 185–186, 207,
    232–233, 244–245, 255, 266, 276
  Adjectives following verbs, 235
  Irregular verbs, 65, 277–278
  Prefixes, 150
  Regular verbs, 166
  Suffixes, 150
  Two-word verbs, 8, 38, 53–54, 64, 105, 142,
    151, 186–187, 205, 256, 265, 278

WRITING
Charts, 108, 162, 174, 183, 224, 233, 254, 281, 285
Compositions, 9, 19, 28, 39, 49, 67, 77, 87, 97,
    106, 121, 131, 142, 152, 162, 176, 188, 197,
    208, 219, 235, 245, 257, 267, 280
Guided writing, 9, 19, 28, 39, 49, 67, 77, 87, 97,
    106, 121, 131, 142, 152, 162, 176, 188, 197,
    208, 219, 235, 245, 257, 267, 280
Lists, 163
Paraphrasing, 94, 138, 184
Reasons for statements, 208
Sentences, 7, 51, 64, 74, 84, 87, 94, 104, 106, 108,
    128, 131, 138, 149, 159, 165, 174, 184, 194,
    197, 204, 216, 232, 235, 242, 254, 257, 264,
    275
Summarizing, 131, 152, 187, 196, 257, 267, 279